SHIFT WORK

SHIFT
WORK

Economic advantages and social costs

Marc Maurice

International Labour Office   Geneva

ISBN 92-2-101095-3

First published 1975

Printed by the International Labour Office, Geneva, Switzerland.

CONTENTS

PREFACE

Shift work is undoubtedly tending to develop rapidly in all industrial countries. The importance that it has already acquired, the prospects that it opens up, but above all the number and diversity of the problems to which it gives rise for employers, workers and the public authorities alike, have led the International Labour Office to include it among the subjects of its research.

This study is intended as a general introduction to the question. It was originally published in French. The author, who is on the staff of the Laboratoire d'économie et de sociologie du travail at Aix-en-Provence and also of the Centre national de la recherche scientifique, adopted a multidisciplinary approach to the subject, and tried to bring out the great diversity of the ways in which shift work can be looked at, whether from the point of view of its extent, the reasons for which it is adopted, the lines along which it is organised or the consequences for the workers that may follow from its use.

The arrangement of the text has been altered, mostly within individual chapters, for English-speaking readers.

INTRODUCTION

The scheduling of hours of work is undoubtedly one of the major social problems of industrial society. As technology advances, the natural rhythm of human life and the pace of industrial production move progressively further apart and become increasingly out of step with one another. This development has been reinforced by other factors, such as urbanisation, and has become one of the features of modern society. New patterns of time utilisation have come into being not only in industry and commerce but also in services. By now, alternating day and night shifts are no longer something that only steel workers, miners or railwaymen have to accept; workers in department stores or theatres, operators and programmers in electronic data processing establishments, air crews and an increasingly large number of workers in the most diverse sectors of industry now also have to work shifts. We are increasingly confronted, in large cities, with a population that is continuously on the move at all hours of the day and even of the night, in contrast to the regular ebb and flow of activities characteristic of the smaller provincial towns. This flexibility in the hours of work almost appears to be contagious: while a car manufacturer may have to make some of his operatives work successive shifts round the clock so that he can rapidly amortise his obsolescent machinery and remain competitive, in large cities the increasing output of vehicles acts as an incentive to the staggering of hours of work so as to reduce traffic congestion; this in turn makes it necessary for certain establishments, such as restaurants, petrol stations, department stores, places of entertainment and public services, to operate more or less continuously.

Thus a new pattern of time utilisation develops, dissociated both from the natural rhythms linked with biological functions and the alternation of day and night, and from the habitual pattern of the working week followed by the weekly period of rest. A development of this kind cannot take place without giving rise to serious problems of individual, community and social welfare, the main issue being how to reconcile natural and legitimate human needs with the technical and economic requirements of a society whose major objective is growth and competitiveness.

The present study, which is concerned with shift work, one of the most widespread ways of arranging hours of work, has been written with these considerations in mind; such shift work may involve one or more shifts employed, whether by day or by night, in establishments whose operations or services may call for continuous working, sometimes even without any break at the weekend.

The spread of this type of arrangement of hours of work, whose origins go back to the beginnings of industrialisation and which calls to mind processes of manufacture that require continuous working for technical reasons, now tends to be mainly due to economic reasons in industrial countries generally: whereas shift working was formerly imposed by purely technical requirements (a blast furnace or a glass melting furnace cannot be shut down), it is now being used increasingly on financial grounds. Technical progress continuously increases the part played by fixed capital investment and depreciation in the determination of costs, and it is well known that in certain cases the rate at which a machine becomes obsolete is greater than that at which it wears out physically; it is therefore necessary to keep all plant and machinery operating at full capacity.

The adoption of shift work nevertheless gives rise to a large number of problems whose solution cannot always be expressed purely in economic terms. Even if the employer can find the manpower he needs (from the point of view both of quantity and of level of skill), he has to consider the extent to which shift work is accepted or rejected by the workers, for whom it may have drawbacks. Most workers in fact regard this method of working as a constraint; moreover, rotating shifts may not only be detrimental to family and social life but may also have harmful effects on health. An evaluation of the profitability of shift work should therefore take into account the human and social costs that are its inevitable consequence.

It will be seen that the study of shift work, with its multiplicity of different aspects, calls for a multidisciplinary approach: it is the concern not only of ergonomists, economists and production engineers but also of sociologists and industrial medical officers. In addition, since this method of organisation also has implications both for the total number of hours worked and for the proportion of night and Sunday work, legislation is necessary in order to ensure the protection and safety of the workers, particularly women and young people.

The various aspects of the subject will be dealt with on the basis of the information available. However, this study will be restricted to the major industrialised countries, and will deal mainly with industrial undertakings: the problems of shift work in the developing countries, or in certain special branches of economic activity such as railways, postal services and telecommunications, and hospitals, will only be mentioned in passing.[1]

In Chapter 1 an endeavour will be made to assess the extent to which work is already organised along these lines and the way in which shift work is tending to develop in different countries. The available statistics are not always such as to make this possible with the degree of precision that would be desirable but the presentation of these figures will make it possible to determine more accurately the scope of this study, and will thus serve as an introduction to the analysis of the main reasons for the adoption and extension of shift work. This latter subject is dealt with in Chapter 2.

Chapter 3 is an examination of the different types of shift work, based on the analysis of the various features that can have an influence on their adoption. That brief review should serve to define the different types, and will aid the understanding of the advantages and disadvantages of each of the systems in use.

Chapters 4 and 5 give an account of the results of the major studies that are known to have been carried out with regard to the effects of shift work on the workers' health and their performance at work, and on their family and social life.

Chapter 6 deals with the attitudes of the workers towards shift work in general and towards particular aspects of it. The preferences expressed by the workers in this connection are not

---

[1] These special aspects of the use of shift work could usefully be the subject of separate studies.

necessarily the same as those of physiologists or of practising members of the medical profession, and they have to be taken into consideration. The study of these attitudes will help in the better understanding of the advantages and drawbacks of the various systems of shift work, and will provide valuable information for persons who shoulder responsibilities in this field.

The institutional factors to be taken into account in the introduction and operation of a shift work system are passed under review in Chapter 7; they include the labour standards applicable in the country concerned, trade union policy and arrangements with regard to staffing, remuneration, communication, supervision and welfare facilities that may help to make it easier for the workers to adapt to the constraints imposed by this method of working.

This study concludes with a provisional assessment of shift work and an account of possible future developments. A number of suggestions, based on various points made in the preceding chapters, are put forward with the aim of pointing the way to improvements in the living and working conditions of shift workers, who constitute an increasingly large proportion of the working population.

Being intended essentially as a general introduction to shift work, this study also includes a number of appendices: in addition to a selected bibliography of the main publications used in its preparation, the appendices give further information on the labour legislation on shift work, examples of the reasons for the adoption of this method of working in various branches of economic activity, examples of different arrangements of hours of work, a number of case studies of the introduction of new systems of continuous working, and statistics.

The aim of this study will have been achieved if it serves to encourage new research to fill the gaps that have been pointed out, and if it succeeds in convincing all persons with responsibilities in this field - particularly employers, trade unionists, industrial medical officers and social workers - that by trying together to discover the best ways of organising shift work they will be dealing with some of the fundamental current and future problems of industrial society, particularly that of reconciling individual preferences and collective choices, social advantage and financial interest.

CHAPTER 1

EXTENT OF SHIFT WORK

It is difficult, with existing sources of statistical data, to
assess the extent to which shift work is done in the various
industrialised countries, and even more difficult to find out how it
is developing. Few systematic and comprehensive studies of the
subject have been undertaken so far, except in France, Japan and
the United Kingdom. Oddly enough, one country that publishes
abundant statistics of all kinds, namely the United States, has not
so far produced any official figures on this subject. The Federal
Republic of Germany has published only the figures from a sample
survey.[1] In most countries, of course, statistics are available
for certain branches of industry, but those statistics are not always
comparable, either because they relate to different periods or because
they are based on different data.

In spite of these difficulties, it is possible to estimate
roughly the relative extent of shift work in the major industrialised
countries, and thereby to demonstrate some of the causes of its
recent extension and probable future development, on the basis of
figures available by branch of industry, branch of economic activity,
and size of undertaking.[2] Thus on the basis of the figures
generally quoted it would seem that the proportion of workers on shift
work over the whole range of industrial activities was 20 per cent
in the United Kingdom in 1964, 21.4 per cent in France in 1963,
12 per cent in Switzerland in 1960, 22 per cent in the Netherlands
in 1959, and, in 1958, 20.4 per cent in Norway, 17 per cent in
Sweden and 13.4 per cent in Denmark. In the United States it was
estimated in 1964-65 that 24.3 per cent of workers in the manufacturing
industries were on shift work.[3] In Japan, in 1968, about 37 per
cent of the workers were on shift work in all the establishments in
which this method of working had been adopted; these constituted
20 per cent of the total number of establishments.

These few figures, together with those quoted later, are given
only as an indication. It is difficult to reach conclusions
applicable to all industrialised countries, in view of the differences
between such countries and the frequent lack of comparable statistical
data: a special study would be necessary in order to determine the
criteria used in each country to define "shift work" and to assess
its extent by branch of economic activity. Certain general state-
ments can, however, be made. Shift work, though originally
restricted to certain industries, seems to have spread considerably
over the last few decades: the frequency of shift work is not
negligible, although it seems to vary considerably. It is now
found in most branches of industry, commerce and service activities,
to such an extent that it appears to be linked with increasing
industrialisation and urbanisation. There are, of course, marked
differences between various branches of industry and between

---

[1] Mikrozensus 1965.

[2] So as not to break the flow of the text, the tables giving
the statistics relied on in this chapter have been placed in an
appendix (4).

[3] See Edward F. Denison: Why growth rates differ (Washington,
Brookings Institution, 1967), p. 152.

establishments of different size; the frequency of shift work also
varies from one country to another.   These differences can be
explained in terms of the economic situation of each industry or
country but they may also be linked to the structure of industry and
employment, to the resistance shown by the workers and by institutions
and organisations such as the churches[1] or the trade unions, and
finally to economic systems.

Relative Frequency of Different Systems

The term "shift work" covers different systems of organisation,
depending on whether there are two or three shifts, whether the
shifts are worked during the day or at night, and again on whether
the work is continuous (without a break at the weekend) or semi-
continuous (with a break at the weekend).   Depending on the circumstances, these major features, which are analysed in more detail
in Chapter 3, may have economic advantages of a varying degree of
importance, but may also constitute constraints of varying extent for
the workers.   The value of statistics that take the various features
of the organisation of shift work into account is therefore obvious,
but sufficiently accurate data of this type are unfortunately
available in only a small number of countries.

Table 1. Percentage of Shift Workers Employed
Under the Main Shift Systems in Use in Industry

	Continuous three-shift system	Semi-continuous three-shift system	Two-shift or other systems	Total
France (1963)	71.0		29.0	100
Japan (1968)	9.0	34.0	57.0	100
Netherlands (1957)	15.3	49.7	35.0	100
United Kingdom (1964)	22.4	18.8	58.8	100

If the most recently published statistics on the subject are
compared (see table 1), it will be seen that most shift workers are
employed under a three-shift system in France and the Netherlands,
whereas most shift workers in Japan and the United Kingdom are
employed under a two-shift system.   Here again, however, the figures

---

[1] This resistance was seen in certain countries, such as the
Federal Republic of Germany and Belgium, when the spread of continuous three-shift working threatened to interfere with the observance
of Sunday as a day of rest, but it seems unlikely that any such
resistance could become widespread in the future.

must be accepted with caution[1]; statistics on the hours of operation
of plant or machinery might indicate more precisely the extent of
continuous work and make it possible to interpret the figures on
shift systems. Nevertheless, it would appear that the continuous
or semi-continuous working of three 8-hour shifts is more widespread
than is generally believed. These differences in organisation, of
course, are closely linked with the type of labour used, i.e. male
or female.

In any case, the frequency of shift work and of the various
systems varies considerably with the size of the undertaking concerned and the branch of industry.

Size of Undertaking

The same general tendency seems to be present in all countries:
the proportion of shift work increases with the size of the
undertaking.[2] Thus the national survey carried out in 1963 in
France showed the proportion of establishments of different sizes
that operated a shift system: in more than a quarter of establishments employing 100 to 199 workers, some of the workers were on
shift work; the proportion rose to nearly half for establishments
with 200 to 999 workers, and to three-quarters for establishments
with 1,000 workers or more. This trend has been confirmed by other
surveys in Japan (1967)[3] and in the United Kingdom and the USSR (1965).
The tendency to introduce shift work for some of the workers thus
seems to be linked with the size of the establishment.

It is interesting to note that the size of the establishment
also influences the proportion of three-shift working, the most
advanced form of shift work; this to some extent strengthens the
validity of the indication given at the beginning of the last
paragraph concerning the general trend. The connection between
establishment size and three-shift working can be observed both in
industry and in the service sector. Thus a survey carried out in
the United States in 1963 in insurance companies showed that not
only does the proportion of shift work increase with the size of
the establishment considered but also that three-shift working
tends to increase with the number of persons employed. In Japan,
however, recently published statistics (1968) appear to show that
the importance of shift work is less closely linked with the size
of the establishment than in other countries. Thus continuous

---

[1] Thus, in the United Kingdom, systems are used that are
operated only to a small extent in other countries, such as alternating day and night shifts, or evening shifts for part-time workers;
such systems are difficult to classify. As far as the Japanese
statistics are concerned, under the heading of continuous work, they
include the working both of three 8-hour shifts and of two 12-hour
shifts.

[2] It should be noted, however, that economic study casts certain
doubts on the notion that there is any necessary link between the two.
See University of Cambridge, Department of Applied Economics: The
economics of capital utilisation: A report on multiple shift work,
by Robin Marris, assisted by Ian Maclean and Simon Bernau, Monographs,
No. 10 (1964, subsequently cited as "Marris").

[3] See appendix 4.

working with three 8-hour shifts is more frequent in undertakings
with fewer than 500 workers, which is contrary to the trend observed
in France and the United Kingdom, for example. In contrast it is
found that the number of workers shows a higher increase with the
size of the undertaking in establishments that have adopted shift
work than it does in industry generally. This trend is also found
in French industry.

Branch of Industry

The extent of shift work also varies with the sector of
economic activity and the industry concerned; together with the
size of the establishment, this is, in fact, one of the main correla-
tions that can be made. If the available statistics on this subject
for various industrial countries (Canada, France[1], Japan[2], and the
United Kingdom) are examined, certain differences between those
countries will of course be found, but the main finding will be one
of similarity among the branches of economic activity and industries
that have adopted shift work.

Among the manufacturing industries, those in which continuous
operation is necessary for technical reasons naturally show the
highest incidence of shift work; such industries include the manufacture of metals and glass, the chemical industry, the oil industry,
and the manufacture of paper and board. These are followed by
industries that have doubtless adopted shift work for economic
reasons, such as the textile industry, the food industry, machine
building and electrical engineering. Depending on the industry,
shift work is either more or less uniformly adopted in establishments
of all sizes, or is more strictly associated with large undertakings
(as in the case of the chemical, oil and textile industries, and
metal manufacture). The number of shifts used also varies with the
industry. Two-shift work is found more often in general engineering,
building, public works, textiles, and leather and hides, while three
shifts are more commonly used in the oil industry, the manufacture
of metals, the chemical industry, and mechanical and electrical
engineering; this suggests that three-shift working may be adopted
as much for technical as for economic reasons.

Proportion of the Sexes in the Workforce

Very few national surveys show the frequency of shift work in
relation to the worker's sex. The information available from France
and the United Kingdom shows that the proportion of women engaged in
shift work is related to the arrangement of hours of work adopted
and to the branch of economic activity concerned.

According to the results of a survey carried out in France in
1957, one-third of all workers engaged in shift work were women;

---

[1] Statistics for 1963; see appendix 4.

[2] Statistics for 1967; see appendix 4.

this is more or less the same as the proportion of women in the
working population.   Nevertheless, of the women who are on shift
work, there is a higher proportion employed under systems of two day
shifts (of 8 hours) or who, as in the United Kingdom, do part-time
work in the evening, after the day shifts are over.   This is no
doubt the consequence of labour legislation under which, with certain
limited exceptions, night work for women is prohibited.[1]

The number of women engaged in shift work is of course linked
to the number of women available for employment in the industry
concerned.   Thus more women than men are found to be on shift work
in the textile industry; they are also present in large numbers,
but are not in the majority, in electrical engineering and the food
industries.[2]

It may be mentioned at this stage that the employment of women
in certain branches of industry raises important problems, since
three-shift working is tending to become more widespread mainly for
economic reasons, and this is gradually leading to a predominance of
men in the labour force.   This development has already been observed
in certain countries, particularly in the textile industry.

General Trends

It is difficult, with the statistics currently available, to
assess the trends in the development of shift work, at least in the
long term.

If, however, the only figures available in this connection,
namely those for France (1957, 1959 and 1963) and for the United
Kingdom (1954 and 1964) are examined, it will be found that in both
countries there is a tendency for shift work to increase.[3]   It is
necessary to distinguish here, however, between the frequency with
which shift work is adopted by industrial establishments and the
number of workers directly affected by this method of working.
Although in both cases, or at least in France, an increase in shift
work is found, it should be noted that in the establishments that

---

[1] It will be noted that in certain countries, such as the
United States, night work by women appears to be commoner than in
France or the United Kingdom.   In the latter two countries,
employers have recently been exerting pressure in favour of a
relaxation of labour legislation in this respect.

[2] Although precise statistics in this field are not available,
it is probable that women are also in the majority in certain postal
services, such as that concerned with the giro or postal cheque
system, and in hospitals, where the work is organised in a different
manner, as compared with the shift systems used in industry, but is
nevertheless subject to the same requirements and restrictions.

[3] Proportion of employees on shift work: France: 1957, 12 per
cent; 1963, 21 per cent; United Kingdom: 1954, 12 per cent;
1964, 20 per cent.   More detailed statistics are given in appendix 4.

have adopted shift work the total number of wage earners has
increased more rapidly than that of the wage earners engaged in
shift work. This may be a consequence of the fact that the number
of wage earners has increased to a smaller extent than that of
salaried employees, and also of the fact that the increases in
productivity obtained through shift work have made it possible to
employ fewer people in the branches of production concerned. The
interpretation of the trends in the development of shift work will
be considered again later, particularly in relation to automation.
Nevertheless, it can be concluded at this stage that, in the medium
term, there is a tendency for shift work to be adopted in an
increasing number of undertakings and establishments, and that it
affects a larger number of workers (both manual and non-manual) than
in the past, although it may be considered that the number of workers
directly affected will not grow in the future at the same rate as at
present, for the reasons that have just been indicated.

It will also be noted, again on the basis of the surveys already
mentioned (France and United Kingdom), that shift work has developed
mainly in the industries in which it was already widespread (manufacture of metals, chemicals, printing, and paper and board). It
would seem, however, that the three-shift system (three 8-hour
shifts) has developed less rapidly than the two-shift system (two
such shifts); this feature is particularly noteworthy in the United
Kingdom, where the greatest increase is seen in permanent night
shifts and in part-time evening shifts, which are combined with two
day shifts.

CHAPTER 2

REASONS FOR ADOPTION AND EXTENSION

Whatever the branch of economic activity or type of industry, the reasons for the adoption or extension of shift work are complex in character, technological and economic factors, in particular, being often interdependent. However, economic reasons would seem to be predominant in the recent tendency towards the extension of this method of working as suggested by the statistics in the previous Chapter. This extension will not necessarily result in an increase in the number of workers on shift work; and in branches of industry in which automation is taking place the increasing proportion of the work carried out under a shift system will not always lead to a proportionate increase in the number of workers affected.

Technological Requirements

Certain types of shift work and night work existed, of course, before the beginning of industrialisation. Shift work as a method of organisation of work and as a social problem, however, dates from the early stages of the development of industries such as iron founding, glass making, lime burning and paper making, in which the nature of the production process makes continuity necessary. The first attempts to regulate this method of working, and to enumerate the activities to which the rules apply, were then apparent in labour legislation.[1] Legislation also provides evidence of the great development of the concept of continuous operation. In France, for example, a decree of 27 October 1936 extended the field of application of that concept to industries "whose operation must, by reason of the nature of the work itself, necessarily continue without interruption at any time of the day, night or week", and an order of 22 June 1937 specified, in addition, that shift work might be adopted for workers in processes that, "although not themselves necessarily continuous in character, are technically dependent on processes that are necessarily continuous". The legislation thus reflects changes in the nature of the work itself and in technological requirements that, little by little, led to the extension of shift working to the most diverse branches of economic activity. The change from the concept of the continuous firing of a furnace or kiln to that of the "continuous nature of the work", and then to that of "technical dependence" on continuous processes, shows that consideration has been given both to purely technological requirements and to those of the organisation of work in increasingly integrated production units: little by little, in addition to technological requirements, there emerged the need to improve the efficiency of the organisation of production so as to achieve maximum returns.

---

[1] See for example, in France, a decree of 31 August 1910, for the implementation of Section 39 of Book II of the Labour Code; the ILO's concern with shift work dates back to its foundation in 1919, as may be seen from the Hours of Work (Industry) Convention, 1919 (No. 1), Articles 2(c), 4 and 5.

To quote only a few examples, although it is obvious that technological requirements make continuous operation necessary in the iron
and steel and chemical industries - a blast furnace or a distillation
column cannot be shut down without giving rise to serious technical
difficulties - it is nevertheless true, even in these industries,
that certain operations could be stopped momentarily without any
great damage, except that the stoppage would lead to a marked
increase in production costs.

Another factor, however, is becoming of increasing importance
in the extension of shift work, namely automation, which can be
considered initially from the technological point of view. One of
the characteristics of automated plant and machinery is that the
manufacturing process is continuous; plant is being increasingly
operated continuously in programmed and automatically controlled
cycles.[1] The period for which a machine is used and the hours of
work of its individual operators are thus no longer the same. In
theory, certain machinery or plant can be operated non-stop, 24 hours
a day; as a result, there is a tendency to arrange for the operatives
to work three 8-hour shifts; but except in the processing of fluids
or gases this is an advanced form of automation that is far from
being generally applicable. Even when automation does not require
the continuous operation of the plant, however, it is not uncommon
for the workers to be organised into two production shifts and a
small maintenance shift. This is also a three-shift system but, in
contrast to the system used for continuous production, only two of
the shifts rotate; the scheduling of the third shift, responsible
for maintenance, is permanent.

Valuable information in this connection has been provided by
the results of an automation survey carried out in France under the
direction of Pierre Naville.[2] The use of automatic machines can
take many forms: the use of such machines may be governed by that of
machines of the traditional type, in which case the automatic machines
are used intermittently or in bursts during the normal working day,
where, as is most commonly the case, any form of synchronisation with
the other machines is impossible; alternatively, if the output of
the automatic machines is less than that of the other machinery,
they will be used for a longer period, exceeding the normal hours of
work; conversely, if the machines of the traditional type are
dependent on the automatic machines, it is probable that there will be
a tendency for them to be used for longer periods, to meet the
requirements of the automated process. Thus, depending on the
situation, the effect of automation on the length of time for which
equipment is used may vary.

_____

[1] See Pierre Naville: Vers l'automatisme social?, Problèmes
du travail et de l'automation (Paris, Gallimard, 1963), p. 229.

[2] Pierre Naville and others: L'automation et le travail humain
(Paris, Centre national de la recherche scientifique (CNRS) 1961);
see also W. Grossin: "Temps-machines, temps-hommes", Cahiers
d'étude de l'automation et des sociétés industrielles (Paris, CNRS),
No. 4, 1962, pp. 171-188, and idem: Le travail et le temps (Paris,
Anthropos, 1969).

The survey showed, in fact, that in one establishment out of four (belonging either to the textile industry or to the electrical and mechanical engineering industry), there was an increase in the length of time for which the plant was used per day after the introduction of an automated process. More generally, it was found that the length of time for which automated equipment was used increased with the complexity of the equipment and the degree of automation of the establishment concerned. Moreover, although the correlation between the degree of automation and the adoption of shift work (two or three 8-hour shifts) was less marked, it was possible to demonstrate a trend that supported the hypothesis[1] that automation, by tending to increase the length of time for which equipment is used, leads to the adoption of shift work once a certain threshold has been passed, namely that corresponding to the possibility of adding on overtime to the normal working day.

It is not possible to conclude, therefore, that a direct link exists between automation and the adoption of shift work. In fact it was found that in some cases after the introduction of automated processes a normal working day of 8 to 10 hours was substituted for two shifts of 8 or 10 hours or three of 8 hours.[2] In addition, where automation has made it necessary to adopt shift working, it also tends to reduce the number of workers employed, while at the same time increasing the volume of production: even if shift work becomes more frequent, the number of workers concerned is not generally greater, in relation to the total number employed in the establishment. It is possible that, in the initial stages, automation may lead to a direct increase in the number of workers on shift work, but that this tendency does not continue at later stages.[3]

It does not seem likely, however, that the technological aspects of automation are by themselves responsible for the increase in the length of time for which plant is used; as stated in the survey just mentioned, it must be recognised that far more than automation as such, causes of a more general character - doubtless economic - determine the length of time for which machines are used, and whether the two-shift, or even the three-shift system is adopted.[4]

---

[1] Naville: L'automation et le travail humain, op. cit., pp. 183-186. The author also pointed out that the lack of precision of the replies to the questionnaire was such that it was not always possible to demonstrate the existence of significant relationships.

[2] A. Lucas: "L'automation à la régie Renault", in Economie et humanisme (Caluire), No. 112, July-August 1958, p. 252; Naville: L'automation et le travail humain, op. cit., p. 398.

[3] W. Grossin points out that although automation may increase the percentage of workers on shift work in the initial stages of its introduction, this does not in any way mean that this tendency will continue when improvements are subsequently made (Le travail et le temps, op. cit., pp. 100-101).

[4] Naville: L'automation et le travail humain, op. cit., pp. 308-309.

Economic Advantage for the Individual Undertaking

There can be no doubt that economic factors are the most important in determining recent developments in shift work. Whereas technological requirements have, in most cases, provided the explanation only for certain sectors, economic reasons, in contrast, concern the whole range of economic activities. In terms of the profitability of the undertaking, the economic arguments in favour of the adoption of shift work can be summarised as follows.[1] If it is assumed that a shift system is adopted, the increased utilisation of capital will tend to increase the profit margins of a company if one or more of the following conditions are satisfied:

- the labour costs are relatively low as compared with the capital costs;

- the expected rate of depreciation of the plant, as a result of the introduction of new techniques, is high;

- the burden of taxation may be reduced by increasing the rate of capital depreciation;

- the adoption of shift work will make it possible to reduce costs;

- supervisory functions are easily split up;

- the average wage of shift workers is not too much greater than that of the other workers;

- the average productivity of shift workers is not markedly lower than that of the other workers;

- the structure of the production process makes it possible for the undertaking to bring a machine into production or take it out without a substantial increase in costs;

- the demand for the firm's products is fairly constant in time, or the cost of storage of finished products is low.

Conversely, if some or most of these conditions are not satisfied, an increased rate of utilisation of capital may well lead to a reduction in the firm's profit margins, or in the extent of the advantage of shift working. Mention may also be made of other conditions put forward, particularly by Marris[2]: narrow range of products, undertakings with the advantage of being the first to use a new technique or to turn out a new product, and availability of manpower in the necessary quantity and quality.

---

[1] From B. J. Jones: "The economic aspects of shift work", in Industrial Welfare Society: Shift work, Information Survey and Report Series, No. 112 (London, Industrial Welfare Society, 1963), pp. 29-30.

[2] Op. cit.

Technological progress itself, of which automation is the most advanced form, continuously increases the importance of fixed capital investment, together with that of depreciation, in the determination of costs. In addition, in certain fields, such progress is so rapid that a machine becomes economically out of date before it is physically worn out; this is what is now well known as "obsolescence". Under these conditions, it is less important to maintain or increase the hours of work of the operatives than to ensure that the machine works as long and as intensively as possible. In view of the fact that the latter, simply because it is highly advanced or complex, is increasingly costly and becomes obsolete increasingly quickly, its rate of depreciation must be calculated not merely, as in the past, on the basis of authorised tax deductions but also with due regard to the rate of technological progress.

The substitution of capital for labour is one of the consequences of technical progress. By an increase in the period of operation of the undertaking, with due regard to the legislation in force in the country concerned, the overheads can be spread over a larger output, and a faster rate of amortisation obtained. Nevertheless, if shift work is adopted on the basis of these considerations, it is also necessary to take into account the additional costs that it involves - more rapid wear and tear in the plant, bonuses and allowances, paid rest pauses, additional supervisory staff, etc. The economic advantage of shift work is obvious, however, as shown by the example put forward by Armin Villiger.[1] According to that author, the difference in the costs per unit of output between an undertaking operating a single shift and that operating with three 8-hour shifts amounts to 17.3 per cent in the case of an investment of 100,000 Swiss francs per work station, and to 38.2 per cent in the case of an investment of 1 million Swiss francs per work station.

One of the examples given by Villiger is shown below (manufacturing cost for the weaving of 100 metres of cloth):

	1 shift	2 shifts	3 shifts
Return on capital	21.05	10.69	7.31
Wage bill	2.41	9.04	9.39
Cost of maintenance of plant (including buildings)	3.43	3.07	2.81
Total costs	32.89	22.80	19.51

It can be seen from these figures that the cost index, based on the figure of 100 for the undertaking operating a semi-continuous[2] system of three 8-hour shifts is 117 for an undertaking working two 8-hour shifts and 168 for one operating for a normal working day.

---

[1] These main arguments are given in his book: Entwicklung und soziale Probleme der industriellen Schichtarbeit, insbesondere in der Schweiz (Winterthur, Verlag Hans Schellenbert, 1967).

[2] As indicated in Chapter 1, the term "semi-continuous" refers to a three-shift system in which the shifts are continuous during the week, but work is stopped at the weekend.

The same calculations, for manufacturing costs in a textile factory and a factory producing machines, give the following indices:

	Textile factory	Machine factory
Three 8-hour shifts (semi-continuous)	100	100
Two 8-hour shifts	109	106
Normal working day	145	144

The differences between the two-shift and the three-shift systems are not very large, but a difference of this size may be of decisive importance in meeting competition.

A survey carried out in the United Kingdom in 1963 covering 225 undertakings in different branches of economic activity showed that 64 per cent used shift work. Out of a total labour force of 88,135 (both manual and non-manual workers), 26 per cent were on shift work. Asked why they had adopted this form of working, 56 per cent of employers replied that it was for economic reasons, mainly to utilise the capital invested in machinery and plant; 28 per cent expected to increase the amount of shift work in the future, while only one thought that the amount of shift work would be reduced as a result of automation.[1] It may be noted that shift work makes it possible to shorten delivery dates, and is sometimes better adapted to external factors such as changes in demand associated with the economic situation or seasonal variations.

Employers sometimes introduce shift working to cope with a reduction in normal hours of work. It is generally agreed that the reduction of hours of work will promote the adoption or development of shift work. The question sometimes arises in terms of overtime. Employers turn to overtime in order to keep up output or to meet increased demand. In view of the cost of overtime, however, it may be preferable, in the long run, to introduce a new shift, since the premiums (bonuses and allowances) paid to shift workers are generally less than this cost. In that case it may be more economic to adopt a system of two 8-hour shifts than to take on additional workers for ordinary day work.

Undoubtedly, a reduction of hours of work can also help to improve the efficiency of rotating shift systems because if shift workers work less than 8 hours per day or 40 per week a larger number of crews must necessarily be formed and will thus be available to operate more advanced systems.

The advantages of shift work for the entrepreneur have been studied in particular by two authors[2] who have attempted to determine the optimum allocation of a given output between two shifts.[3]

---

[1] Industrial Society: Shift work: Current practice in Great Britain, Information Survey and Report Series, No. 140 (London, 1966).

[2] K. J. W. Alexander and John Spraos: "Shift working: An application of the theory of the firm", in Quarterly Journal of Economics (Cambridge, Massachusetts, Harvard University), Vol. 70, No. 4, Nov. 1956, p. 605.

[3] The allocation that reduces the total cost of the output to a minimum.

They showed that, if the two shifts have the same marginal cost curve (a U-shaped curve, with output measured along the horizontal axis), and if, in addition, both shifts operate in the rising part of the curve, the optimum is reached when the marginal costs of the two shifts are equal. That is not so, however, if they operate in the falling part of the curve. If one of the shifts operates in the rising part of the curve and the other in the falling part, the optimum depends on the respective slopes of those two parts of the curve; nevertheless, if in this case the total output can be increased (instead of attempting to find the optimum allocation of a given output), the level of operation of each shift will be brought nearer the minimum point of its marginal cost curve. Comparing, by analogy, the position of a firm with two single-shift plants with that of a firm with only one plant but operating a two-shift system, they show the superiority of the second arrangement as compared with the first, as far as the cost of buildings and obsolescence are concerned. They note that on the other hand the transport costs of a two-plant firm may be lower.

Macro-economic Advantages

A major advantage of shift work from the point of view of the national economy as a whole is that its adoption may result in a reduction in unemployment, or may provide work for those potentially unemployed. In some cases the choice may be between shift work or no work at all. Shift work may also be attractive to women for whom normal day work was seriously inconvenient.

Besides its role in promoting full employment, the main macro-economic advantage of shift work is that it enables fuller use to be made of capital goods.

Surveys such as that carried out by the prices directorate of the French Ministry of the National Economy have shown that in a number of branches of economic activity in France there was not a shortage but an excess of machinery; idle machines may act as a brake on economic expansion and reduce competitiveness on the world market.[1] In many countries modern machines, designed to operate throughout the year (i.e. for over 8,700 hours) without any stoppages except for maintenance, are often operating for only 2,000 hours a year, and sometimes even less.[2] This situation must obviously have repercussions on costs and prices. The under-utilisation of machines is no doubt part of the reason why, in many branches of industry, the same machines used on opposite sides of the Atlantic

---

[1] The following is an example taken from the textile industry: the average length of time of operation of a spindle was 3,920 hours a year in France in 1958-59, as compared with 4,680 hours in Belgium, 4,850 hours in Japan, 6,340 hours in the United States, 6,800 hours in India and Pakistan and 8,455 hours in Hong Kong.

[2] Jean Fourastié: La productivité (Paris, Presses universitaires de France, 1962), p. 100.

give results that are so different from the point of view of the consumer; it is not unusual to find that, with the same machines, the cost price can vary by a factor of two.[1]

The economic consequences of the under-utilisation of machinery and plant are even more marked in the event of automation. It is stressed, in the majority of the studies concerned with the effects of technical progress, that the beneficial effects of automation cannot be fully achieved unless the equipment is used intensively, because of the high cost of the plant.[2] It was shown, in addition, in surveys previously mentioned which were directed by P. Naville, that a link exists between the degree of automation, the complexity of the machine tools and the period for which the equipment is used.[3]

This is a logical consequence of the economics of the situation which cannot fail to contribute to the extension of shift work. While this is true of all branches of industry or economic activity, it is particularly noticeable in industries where there is both a high rate of capital investment and constantly changing products or methods of production. This applies especially to the chemical industry (for heavy chemicals, investment sometimes amounts to nearly twice the annual turnover, and plant must frequently be renewed[4]), the automobile industry (it is estimated that 60 to 70 per cent of the machines used in this industry are obsolete before they are worn out, so that rapid amortisation is necessary since the commercial life of any particular model is becoming increasingly short), and the textile industry (modernisation since the Second World War in this industry has led to a marked increase in shift work, including night work[5]).

Alexander and Spraos[6] argue that from the point of view of the economy as a whole, the introduction of shift work, by reducing the stock of capital required to produce a given output, can encourage the entry of new firms into an industry and thus makes the economy more competitive, provided, however, that the firms already established in the industry do not also resort to this method of working. This conclusion is no longer valid, however, if economies of scale are reaped in the form of lower average variable costs[7]; it is valid

---

[1] Fourastié, op. cit. p. 100.

[2] Communauté économique européenne (CEE) Progrès technique et Marché commun (Brussels, 1960), vol. 1, p. 234.

[3] Grossin: "Temps-machines, temps-hommes", op. cit., p. 185.

[4] See, in particular: "Shift work and overtime in the chemical industries", in International Labour Review (Geneva, ILO), Vol. LXXXI, No. 6, June 1960, pp. 557-565.

[5] "Labour problems of modernisation in the textile industry", ibid., p. 527.

[6] Alexander and Spraos, op. cit.

[7] There is no advantage in employing two shifts in an establishment which, in terms of equipment, falls short of the size that will reduce average variable costs to a minimum.

only if the benefits of large-scale production lie in the spread of
overheads over a large output.

The authors also point out that, to the extent that shift work
reduces the useful life of capital equipment (thus rendering these
"durable" goods less durable), it contributes towards reducing the
cyclical bunching of replacement demand and thereby towards the
stabilisation of the economy.

In regard to the question of better use of capital, let us
take the case of an industrialised economy with a certain stock of
capital, used annually for a certain number of hours with labour
working a normal day whose duration, for a normal wage rate, is
fixed either by law or by collective agreement. The number of
hours of operation of the existing capital can be increased in the
following two different ways. First, the number of hours of work
per worker can be increased, either by means of daily or weekly
overtime or by means of additional days per year. This method of
increasing the period of operation of the equipment, however, soon
reaches the quantitative limit imposed by the law or the qualitative limit resulting from decreased productivity in the last few
hours of a work period. Alternatively, a certain amount of shift
working can be introduced. A distinction should be drawn here
between the following two cases.

(1) If the number of workers is excessive in relation to the existing capital, the introduction of shift work will make it
possible, besides increasing the number of hours of capital
utilisation, to make better use of some of the workers previously underemployed. This new distribution of the work
over time will be reflected in an improvement in the productivity of both capital and labour.

(2) If the existing capital is fully utilised in the context of
the single shift, an increase in the degree of utilisation of
that capital will be obtained by increasing the number of
workers employed and introducing multiple shifts. This presupposes that manpower is available, or in other words a situation in which the existing capital in the economy is not
sufficient to provide employment, under a single-shift system,
for the whole of the available working population. The adoption of a multiple-shift system will make it possible, in this
case, to increase the employment capacity of the economy[1] and
the productivity of the capital stock. It will be seen,
therefore, that even on the assumption of a constant stock of
fixed assets, the adoption of a multiple-shift system leads
to the improved utilisation not only of capital but also of
labour. Nevertheless, these effects will be obtained only if
the change yields a sufficiently high level of profit. It is
necessary, therefore, to consider the effects of the adoption
of a shift system on production costs.

---

[1] On the assumption that the level of skills is satisfactory
and that the vocational training system is adequate to meet new
demands.

Labour Costs

The use of a shift system results in an increase in the total wages bill because of the increase in the number of workers employed, and also in a rise in labour cost per worker, for three reasons.

The premiums paid for shift work constitute the most obvious of these reasons. As pointed out in a monograph of the Department of Applied Economics of the University of Cambridge[1], the size of these premiums is in some degree dependent on the extent to which shift working is prevalent in the economy; that itself determines to some extent the workers' own evaluations of such factors as the difficulty of obtaining transport at unusual hours, domestic problems and the difficulty of getting used to sleeping during the day, only the workers' instinctive dislike of night work being a genuinely independent factor. If we adopt the term used in the Cambridge monograph[2] of "economic resistance" to shift work for the increase in the average hourly wage rate resulting from the change from a single-shift system to one with several shifts, then the higher the proportion of wages in the total costs and the greater the ratio of wages to profits, the greater the influence of this resistance will be.

A second reason arises from the nature of the work force employed, and is found mainly in establishments that make use principally of female labour. Night work by women or young people is usually prohibited, either by law or by collective agreement. For such establishments, therefore, the adoption of a shift system also means the employment of a male labour force, usually paid at a rate higher than that for women workers.

A third reason, whose effects supplement those of the two preceding ones, is the increasing shortage of labour that results from an increase in the number of shifts, particularly where the existing assets are sufficient to provide employment on a single-shift basis to the majority of the available working population.[3]

In the Cambridge monograph it was suggested[4], on the basis of a 1951 survey of the manufacturing industries, that a doubling of the rate of capital utilisation (number of hours of operation per year) was associated with an increase of between 20 and 30 per cent in the hourly cost of labour (annual average).

The difference observed between rates of pay may, however, be over-estimated in certain cases (the establishments where multiple-shift systems are used are fairly large and can offer normal wages that are higher than the average for industry as a whole) and under-estimated in others (workers on shift work often have shorter weekly hours of work).

---

[1] Marris, op. cit., pp. 20-21.

[2] Ibid., pp. 24-25.

[3] For unskilled work, however, immigration of labour may prevent or eliminate a shortage.

[4] Marris, op. cit., p. 139.

The repercussions of the adoption of a multiple-shift system on labour costs are therefore difficult to calculate on the basis of the over-all statistics available.

Capital Costs

The increase in operating time makes it possible to reduce capital costs per unit of output or, for the same costs, to increase the rate of amortisation; the higher the proportion of the total costs accounted for by the fixed costs (interest, amortisation), the greater the effect will be. As far as maintenance costs are concerned, some of these are also fixed costs. The others vary with the extent of use and tend to increase faster with older machines. In an economy where technical progress results in rapid obsolescence, however, machines become technically obsolete before they are physically worn out. As a consequence, the proportion of variable maintenance costs is not higher, for the same output, when a shift system is used. For these various reasons, therefore, the faster the rate of obsolescence the more obvious the economic advantage of multiple-shift working.

There is a reciprocal interaction between the rapidity of obsolescence and the adoption of a shift system which must be pointed out: obsolescence due to technical progress stimulates the more intensive use of capital, which in turn speeds up obsolescence. This interaction between obsolescence and shift work tends to have cumulative effects. When shift work is adopted initially only by certain undertakings in an industry, they have the advantage of a better use of capital than the others; since the demand for new machines remains small, however, the rate of obsolescence is also low, and they find, after a time, that their variable maintenance costs are increasing. However, if, because of competition, they reduce their prices before that time, the other undertakings will also adopt the shift system. The demand for new machines will then increase, and with it the rate of obsolescence. Fast obsolescence will make shift work even more profitable, since the maintenance costs of the plant will no longer be increased by the effects of mere ageing. The prevalence of shift work and the rate of technical progress will increase simultaneously.

An increased prevalence of shift work may thus be due to purely economic causes. It must be asked, however, whether a threshold exists above which an increase in the degree of utilisation of capital is no longer profitable to the economy. In order to answer this question, it is necessary to take labour into account, since it is not always available in unlimited amounts.

Towards an Optimum System

As already indicated, the adoption of a shift system has the effect of increasing employment capacity, and consequently the relative scarcity of labour. If, however, there is new investment that leads to a saving of labour, it can compensate for that scarcity.

The adoption of a shift system therefore makes it possible to combine, in an optimum pattern, a high degree of utilisation of capital, thereby increasing its productivity, with increased capital investment, which tends to increase labour productivity for a given working population. If the available working population is too

large in relation to the employment provided by a given stock of
capital, net new investment can be made at such a rate that it will
be possible not only to absorb the population available for work
but also, thanks to the higher quality of the new capital, to
operate a two-shift system and thus to double the efficiency of production and of its factors.

Another advantage results from the fact that the increase in
productivity obtained makes it possible to reduce the hours worked
per worker employed, without any decrease in output. The reductions are, in practice, combined with increases in hourly wage
rates. Profits will be protected, however, if the increase in
hourly wage rates does not exceed the increase in productivity, the
more so since a reduction in the number of hours worked per opera-
tive does not involve a proportionate decrease in output.

Size and Specialisation

When what may be called innovative potential is considered in
relation to the increased utilisation of capital resulting from the
adoption of a multiple-shift system, one is led to inquire which
type of undertaking is in the best position to introduce such a
system. In particular, is there a relationship between the size
of undertakings and shift work?

Competition among private firms may lead to the division of
the market among a large number of medium-sized undertakings in
spite of the fact that from the technical point of view a small
number of large undertakings would be more efficient. The consumer
is then offered a very wide range of products, which reduces the
market share of each undertaking, and thus restricts both the out-
lets and the possibility of increasing output and, as a result, the
increased utilisation of capital. In addition, the adoption of
shift work requires additional executive, supervisory and technical
staff and gives rise to an additional burden on management -
inversely proportionate to the size of the undertaking.

In the United Kingdom it has been calculated, on the basis of
the 1951 census of production, that in manufacturing, 6 per cent of
undertakings employing 80 per cent of the workers on shift work,
produced 25 per cent of the total net output.[1] Of the 128 industries considered, 38 did not include a single establishment operating a multiple-shift system, and the size of these establishments
was relatively small. In 9 out of 10 of the remaining industries,
the ratio of average net output per establishment making most use
of shift work (proportion of the workers on shift work greater than
35 per cent) to the corresponding average in the establishments
making less use of such work (less than 35 per cent of their
workers) was greater than 101 per cent, and the unweighted mean
given in the Cambridge monograph for all the industries in question
is 220 per cent.[2]

If output is taken as the criterion of the size of an undertaking, it would therefore seem that the greater the size the more
shift working is used. However, the average number of workers

---

[1] Marris, op. cit., p. 136.

[2] Ibid., p. 149.

employed by the establishments in which shift work was most extensively used was 15 per cent less than in the establishments where it
was used less extensively.[1] What is the explanation for this
apparent divergence between the results, depending on whether output or numbers employed is taken as the criterion of size?

A section of the glass industry in Great Britain, viz. "glass
other than containers"[2], is a good example of this situation. Of
the 300 establishments surveyed, 16 per cent accounted for 75 per
cent of the net output, but employed only 70 per cent of the
workers. These establishments had the most capital-intensive
methods of production, paid the highest wages, and obtained the
highest labour productivity, but manufactured only one fairly homo-
geneous product, namely flat glass. The others, where multiple-
shift systems were not worked, were less highly mechanised and
manufactured a wide variety of products. The general conclusion
can be drawn from these results that the undertakings in which
shift working is most profitable are those turning out one or two
uniform products so that both a high degree of mechanisation and a
fairly simple organisation of production are possible.[3]

If, therefore, an attempt is made to relate the extent to
which shift working is adopted to the size of the undertaking,
account must be taken of size expressed not only in terms of number
of workers employed but also of output, and allowance must be made
for the degree of uniformity of the product and the nature of the
demand.

Application to a Developing Economy:
Case of the Socialist Countries

These arguments, which have so far been developed in the context of a growing industrialised economy, should also be taken into
consideration in any discussion of the advantages of this type of
organisation of work for a developing economy. In articles dealing with six Eastern European countries, M. Kabaj gives examples of
the increase in employment resulting from the adoption of shift
work.[4] The index of capital utilisation, which the author calls
the shift coefficient, is defined as the ratio between the number of
man-days worked and the number of man-days worked on the main
(first) shift. An increase in this ratio indicates an increased
use of shift work.

---

[1] Ibid., p. 150.

[2] Flat glass plus domestic and fancy glassware (e.g. domestic
drinking glasses, heat-proof glass cooking utensils, decorative
fruit bowls, glass vases, salt cellars, ash trays), scientific and
optical glass, electric light bulbs and other miscellaneous non-
flat glass products. The gross value of sales of these non-flat
products was as great as that of flat glass.

[3] Marris, op. cit., pp. 172-177.

[4] M. Kabaj: "Shift work and employment expansion", in International Labour Review, Vol. 91, No. 1, Jan. 1965, pp. 47-62;
idem: "Shift work and employment expansion: Towards an optimum
pattern", ibid., Vol. 98, No. 3, Sept. 1968, pp. 245-274.

The shift coefficient increased by 18.5 per cent in the USSR over the period 1928-1932, by 24 per cent in Hungary from 1950 to 1954, and by 19 per cent in Poland from 1951 to 1958.   The most striking increases and the highest percentages were found in mechanical engineering, chemicals and textiles.   During the periods in question, the increase in employment resulting from this increased utilisation amounted to 59 per cent in Hungary, 48 per cent in Poland and 33 per cent in the USSR.

On the assumptions of full employment, an unlimited demand for products, and the absence of restraints on the expansion of production, Kabaj considers that a double-shift system is the optimum; experience gives, in fact, an optimum coefficient in the range 1.6 to 1.8, which in certain cases may lead to the elimination of the night shift.[1]   In the light of this optimum and of the coefficients observed for industry as a whole around 1963, the author describes the employment expansion opportunities that may result from an increase in the shift coefficient.[2]

Since the achievement of a maximum profit is not an essential purpose of undertakings in the Socialist countries, the working of two day shifts may be considered in cases in which, in industrialised countries with a market economy, competition would make it necessary to introduce a night shift in addition.

On the other hand, from the macro-economic point of view, the desire to increase output and employment to the greatest possible extent, at least in the initial stages of the development of the Socialist countries, was a possible inducement for the introduction of shift work.   In the second stage, now in progress, when these objectives of the maximisation of output and employment lose some of their importance as a result of increases in output already achieved and the attainment of full employment, the optimum is determined by social objectives in combination with economic objectives.

Public Services and Amenities

The factors considered so far have been technological and economic, but the development of shift work may also be affected by other factors.   One need only mention urbanisation, which increasingly requires the continuous or semi-continuous operation of a whole range of public or private services, including those responsible for communications (postal services, telegraph, telephone), the provision of information (radio, television), or public transport (railways, motor coach and bus services, airlines and shipping companies);   power generation (electricity, gas, nuclear power);   health services (clinics, hospitals);   safety and security (firemen, ambulance men, police, watchmen, surveillance);   or places of entertainment (cinemas, theatres, gambling houses) and restaurants.   This list is not complete, since urbanisation has a

---

[1] See in this connection the experience acquired in the textile industry in the USSR.   Kabaj: "Shift work and employment expansion: Towards an optimum pattern", op. cit., pp. 262-265.

[2] Ibid., Appendix II, pp. 269-273.

kind of contagious effect on the opening or operating times of an
ever-increasing number of establishments or services. In order to
extend service hours beyond normal hours of work or to provide continuous service, it has gradually been necessary to introduce a
system of successive or overlapping shifts, often organised on a
different basis from those used in industry.

A further effect of urbanisation on hours of work is that of
the daily and weekly peaks that are a feature both of traffic or
transport in general and of energy consumption. Such anomalies
have been shown to be very costly to the national economy. Many
of the studies carried out in this field call for the staggering of
hours of work and of the timing of various activities in large
urban areas. The solutions suggested include the continuous working day, in which a break of half an hour or an hour is substituted
for the traditional break between noon and 2 p.m., and the extension
of shift work, particularly in the form of two 8-hour shifts.
This is an example of "voluntary" staggering of the timing of
activities with the aim of solving a problem that is both economic
(the peaks in the use of transport and in energy consumption impose
a heavy cost burden on the economy of a country), and social in
character (the increasingly difficult living and working conditions
in large cities are one of the main causes of worker fatigue).

CHAPTER III

CHOICE OF SYSTEMS

In the light of the numerous reasons for its adoption, shift work must be seen no longer as an isolated aspect of economic and social life but as a way of life that is tending to become more widespread throughout industrial society. Although it still affects only a relatively small proportion of the workers, it deserves attention since the study of the problems that it now raises contributes to the development of patterns for the distribution of working and leisure time in the society of the future. Before the consequences of shift working are considered, however, it is necessary to study the main types of shift systems and their sometimes considerable beneficial or harmful effects on the individual and the community.

A distinction is usually made between successive shift work and "normal day work". In the latter case, which is that of the majority of workers, work is carried out during the day, most commonly during two periods, the first in the morning and the second in the afternoon, separated by a lunch break of one or two hours.[1]

Each worker thus continues on the following day the work begun the day before. The position is not the same with shift work, since one shift is followed by the next, each one taking over from the other, and continuing the work begun by the preceding shift. The essential feature of this latter method of working is precisely the continuity of production and the lack of continuity of the work performed by each individual worker. In the extreme case of a factory operating round the clock, the machines operate continuously, while one shift follows another for successive periods of 8 hours, thus achieving continuous production. When, for example, a worker is a member of the morning shift, he continues the work begun before his arrival by a worker on the night shift. However, continuity may mean different things depending on the circumstances: production may be truly continuous, as in the case of a steel works or an oil refinery, or may require only a certain degree of continuity, e.g., for a number of days during the week but with a break at the weekend, or for two-thirds of the day only, with a break during the night.

Differing requirements, which may be, as already pointed out, technical or economic in character, imply differing methods of organising shift work and give rise to different arrangements of work schedules. Thus truly continuous operation requires the work to be organised in three successive shifts of 8 hours each, so as to cover the 24 hours of the day. If operation can be stopped at the weekend, semi-continuous working with three 8-hour shifts will be adopted. Depending on production requirements, the day may also be divided up between two successive shifts; this system of two 8-hour shifts is the one most commonly used; it does not require a night shift, as do the systems previously mentioned.

---

[1] It should be noted, in this connection, that there is a tendency to go over to a "continuous working day", which involves 8 hours (or more) of work with only a short break (varying from half to three-quarters of an hour) in the middle of the day. These hours of work enable workers, particularly in large towns, to leave work earlier and to have a longer evening. Lunch is then often eaten in a canteen or restaurant, either in the undertaking or close to it.

Those are the main types of shift work most commonly found in industry or in certain services. Their main features will now be described and the opportunities for innovation in this field will be stressed. (Such work is often considered only in terms of its economic benefits, but it continues to give rise to personal inconvenience. The description in subsequent chapters will explain the need for innovations.)

The organisation of shift work increased in complexity in going from the two-shift system to the discontinuous three-shift system, i.e., with a break at the weekend, and finally to the continuous system, also involving three shifts every 24 hours but covering the seven days of the week. A distinction will be made between these various systems, both to show how they are organised and to bring out subsequently their various advantages and drawbacks, but no attempt will be made to give a complete description of the large number of possible arrangements of shifts, as in the case, for example, of continuous working with three 8-hour shifts. However, for each system the most recently used variations will be mentioned when they are of special interest. It will thus be seen that the various shift systems allow, to a greater extent than is usually believed, a fairly wide margin of choice, each system having, for the workers, a series of advantages and drawbacks that should be taken into account by those responsible for decisions in this respect.

The Two-Shift System

This is undoubtedly, according to the statistics available for various countries, the most commonly used system in the majority of economic activity, whether in industry, commerce or the service sector. It is the system that appears to be the most acceptable to the workers, since it causes less disturbance to them, their families and the community. The opportunities for increasing the number of hours worked provided by the two-shift system, either by changing the length of each shift or by arranging for part of the weekend to be worked, no doubt explains employers' preference for it, provided that technical considerations do not compel them to go over to three 8-hour shifts.

The two-shift system, in fact, enables the daily hours of work to be used in a very flexible manner; the number of hours worked may vary, for each shift, from 8 to 12 hours, depending on production requirements. Most commonly operated during the day (for example, first shift from 6 a.m. to 2 p.m., second shift from 2 p.m. to 10 p.m.), it avoids night work as far as possible, that being one of the major difficulties connected with the system of three 8-hour shifts. As under other shift systems a break, which may vary from half an hour to 40 minutes, is allowed in each shift to enable the workers to eat a meal. This period is generally included in the hours of work for purposes of remuneration, and the effective length of the working day is therefore reduced. It should be noted that the extension of the length of the shifts beyond 8 hours may run into difficulties in the case of women workers, since night work by women is restricted by law.

The main differences among two-shift schemes relate to starting and stopping times, rotating or non-rotating shifts, and Saturday working.

Starting and Stopping Times

Starting and stopping times vary from undertaking to undertaking, region to region, and country to country. These differences are the result either of variations in the economic situation (need to increase the number of hours worked in order to meet increased demand), or of ways of life typical of certain regions or countries. Thus in urban areas the starting time of the morning shift is generally later than in rural or less urbanised areas. In large towns, undertakings have to take account of the times at which public transport services operate; the morning shift then most commonly starts work between 5 a.m. and 6.30 a.m., whereas in small provincial towns or in undertakings located in rural areas the morning shift may start between 3.30 a.m. and 5 a.m. One French heavy metallurgical company arranges the timing of its two-shift system as follows: 3.45 a.m., 11.45 a.m. and 7.45 p.m. The majority of the workers in this factory, which is located in a rural area, have links with the countryside and continue to work on the land; this routine gives them a complete half-day and a satisfactory evening. It is true that in this case most of the workers live near the factory. Undertakings must take into account the distance that the workers have to travel between home and work, the available means of transport and, in some cases, the possibility of using their own transport services to bring the workers in. It can also happen, however, that the public transport system is obliged to adapt itself to the hours of work of the company; thus, in Turin, the number of workers employed in the car industry is so large that the public transport system has to adapt its services to changes in the hours of work of the company concerned.

Rotating or Non-rotating Shifts

In general, a scheme of two 8-hour shifts is arranged on the basis of a weekly rotation: the workers alternate between the morning shift and the afternoon shift, and the changeover takes place at the beginning of each week. Other arrangements exist, however, under which either there is no alternation of shifts or the length of the cycle of rotation exceeds one week. In the first case, we have a system of non-rotating shifts: the workers remain permanently on the morning or the afternoon shift. This system is used in the United Kingdom and the United States, and also in France. In the United States, some works contracts specify that length of service gives a worker the right to change his shift. In France this system has been adopted in a few undertakings, particularly in the textile industry.

Under systems of rotating shifts the length of the cycle of rotation may vary; it may be one week, which is the commonest arrangement, but also a fortnight, a month, or three months. In certain countries, such as the United States, long cycles of rotation seem to be more frequent than in Europe; but fortnightly alternation is also found in France, the Federal Republic of Germany and the United Kingdom, although the reason for the adoption of the system is not always apparent. It is most commonly the result of local customs based on past experience, or the expression of certain resistance to change.

The frequency of alternation may also vary within the same undertaking, different arrangements being used for workers and supervisors respectively. In the case of the latter, a frequency of alternation greater than that of the workers makes it possible for the same supervisor to supervise all the shifts in succession, thus avoiding the situation in which a supervisor has only one shift to look after. Certain employers may incidentally be afraid that too strong a feeling of solidarity may develop between workers and supervisory staff in such a situation.

Saturday Work

Saturday work clearly has the same effects as varying the length of each shift; it is a method of increasing or decreasing the length of the working week, depending on economic requirements. With a five-day working week, both for the morning and for the afternoon shift, the number of hours worked on each shift is generally greater than 8; the number of hours worked on one of the shifts, for example the afternoon shift, is sometimes increased so as to obtain an average working week of more than 40 hours. This system has been adopted in the car industry in the Federal Republic of Germany, while in France, in the same industry, the system most commonly adopted is that whereby the morning shift works six days a week and the afternoon shift works five. In certain other cases some of the workers, for example those on maintenance work, are obliged to work on Saturday, or even on Sunday, their weekly day of rest then being another day of the week.

Other Variations

Some variations on the most commonly used two-shift system may be noted here, namely the system frequently used in the United Kingdom of day and night shifts, and the system of shifts working less than 8 hours, which can also be combined with the normal work schedule (split shift).

The British system is generally adopted because of the organisational flexibility associated with it. It involves a day shift working, for example, from 7.30 a.m. to 4.30 p.m., or from 8 a.m. to 5 p.m. (including a 1-hour break between noon and 1 p.m.), and a night shift working, for example, from 9 p.m. to 6 a.m. Such a system makes it easy to increase the number of hours worked per day by the use of overtime, while the gap between the day shift and the night shift can be used for maintenance purposes. The flexibility of this system has made it very attractive to British industry, by which it is more widely used than the traditional system of two successive 8-hour shifts. As with the latter, there may or may not be rotating arrangements; the absence of such arrangements may make it possible, in certain cases, to use both male and female labour, the night shift workers then being exclusively men.

Another variant of the two-shift system may also be mentioned: in addition to two alternating day shifts (morning and afternoon), made up of women, a night shift of male workers is sometimes used, possibly working only a few days a week, usually including the weekend. This arrangement, which is often adopted in the United Kingdom, gives a certain degree of continuity, without, however, requiring the continuous three-shift system.

Yet another variation consists in using, in addition to workers on normal work schedules, a shift that works for two periods of the day separated by a gap of a few hours; these two periods may sometimes be worked by different workers, who then work only a limited number of hours per day. This system, known as the split shift, is designed to deal with a rush of work at certain times of the day, such as occurs in certain commercial undertakings or public services (public transport, banking, telecommunications, etc.). It also makes it possible to employ workers who wish to work only a few hours a day, as in the case of women looking for part-time work.

Thus, although the two-shift system is less complex than the system of three continuous 8-hour shifts, it offers quite a range of opportunities for variation. Its most distinctive features are precisely its flexibility and the fact that, in general, it does not involve working throughout the night. Certain employers have adopted it in order to keep down the cost of overtime while increasing the productivity of their machines or plant, whereas others may prefer it to the three-shift system precisely because overtime can be worked with it when the need arises.

The Semi-Continuous Three-Shift System

With a system of three 8-hour shifts, the arrangement of the hours of work becomes both more rigid and more complex. A distinction must be made between semi-continuous working (with work easing at the weekend) and continuous working without a weekend break. This distinction, as will be seen later, is very important, since the possibility of using three-shift systems depends on this, to some extent.

The semi-continuous system will be considered first, since its organisational problems are relatively simple by comparison with those associated with continuous working. This system involves three shifts - a morning shift, an afternoon shift and a night shift - each shift being worked for five or six days a week. The length of the weekend break varies depending on the particular shift and on the direction of rotation.

The system has been adopted for technical reasons where a production cycle lasts longer than 24 hours (as in the chemical industry, cement works, ceramics factories and certain sections of the iron and steel industry) although the processes are not, strictly speaking, continuous, or for economic reasons, to meet increased demand (for which purpose the three-shift system may be adopted on a temporary basis), or to reduce costs; one of its advantages, in addition, is the possibility of working a few hours of overtime at the weekend.

The only possible variations under this system relate to the direction of rotation, the number of shifts per week and the frequency of rotation or change of shift.

Direction of Rotation

The direction of rotation provides the basis for distinguishing between two semi-continuous systems of three 8-hour shifts - the

normal system and the inverted system. Under the former, the
workers move, in succession, from the morning shift to the afternoon
shift, and then to the night shift, and repeat the same cycle as the
weeks pass. Under the latter, the order of shift rotation is the
opposite: the workers move from the afternoon shift to the morning
shift, from the morning shift to the night shift, and finally from the
night shift to the afternoon shift. As we shall see later, the two
directions of rotation affect the length of the rest period under
the continuous system; in the case of the semi-continuous system,
by contrast, the variations are more qualitative in character, since
the change from the night shift to the morning shift may be felt to
be more of a strain than that from the night shift to the afternoon
shift, as has been shown by certain studies that will be referred to
later. If these psychophysiological considerations are left on one
side, the adoption of one or other of the systems does not seem to be
based on any particular requirements - notably technical requirements -
related to the organisation of work. The two systems can coexist in
the same undertaking, but in different departments.

Number of Shifts

     Another variable is the number of shifts per week and the number
of hours worked on the last shifts of the week. The commonest system
requires the morning shift to work six days a week (for example, from
6 a.m. on Monday to 2 p.m. on Saturday), the afternoon shift to work
five days a week (for example, from 2 p.m. on Monday to 10 p.m. on
Friday), and the night shift also to work five days a week (for
example, from 10 p.m. on Monday to 6 a.m. on Saturday). A total of
128 hours of work is thus obtained, corresponding to an average of
42 hours and 40 minutes for each crew.[1] It is possible, where
necessary, to work one additional afternoon shift and one night shift,
so as to obtain 144 hours of work a week, corresponding to an average
of 48 hours, or again to make one or other of the shifts work for more
or less than 8 hours at the end of the week. This is done, for
example, in undertakings using computers that operate for 37 or
37 1/2 hours a week, depending on the workload. The advantage of a
semi-continuous three-shift system is precisely this flexibility,
which makes it possible to increase or decrease the average weekly
number of hours of work while keeping all or almost all of Sunday
free thanks to the break at the weekend.

Frequency of Rotation

     One last factor provides opportunities to vary this system,
namely the frequency of rotation: crews generally change shift every
week, but other arrangements exist whereby the changeover takes place
every fortnight or every month.

---

[1] In the example given, the morning shift works 48 hours a week
and the two other shifts 40.

The Continuous Three-Shift System

With the continuous three-shift system, the full complexity of working with consecutive shifts is encountered. No attempt will be made to describe all existing systems, and still less all possible systems; an account will be given, however, of those that are most frequently used, and of some of the organisational principles whereby new systems can be developed.

Before the main systems are analysed, it is worth considering their usual elements. Those of greatest significance include the number of crews used, the frequency of change of shift, the direction of rotation, the length of the cycle of rotation, the number of consecutive hours of rest and the way in which those hours are distributed over the cycle, and the number of free Sundays in the cycle.

It is thanks to the variation in these factors that it is possible to arrange numerous systems of rotation such that continuous operation is possible throughout the 168 hours of the week. The possibility of changing from one system to another will depend, however, on the average daily number of hours of work that each shift performs or is desired to perform. In order to obtain the desired weekly number of hours, it is sometimes necessary to require crews to work a shift corresponding to normal day work (for example, 8 a.m. to 4 p.m., or 8 a.m. to noon and 2 to 6 p.m.). Such systems are known as mixed systems, and will be described in a later section.

Frequency of Change of Shift

The frequency of change of crews among the various shifts vary from two days to a fortnight or more. Weekly changeovers are the commonest, and as will be seen below this may in fact correspond simply to a period of working five or six days of work performed between two rest periods. Weekly changeovers of shift would seem to be a compromise between a short cycle of rotation (two or three days) and a long cycle (a fortnight or a month); but they fit in, above all, with one of the conventional alternations of work and leisure in modern society.

Direction or Sequence of Rotation

Shifts may rotate in chronological order (morning, afternoon, night) or in the opposite direction (night, afternoon, morning). This affects the distribution of the hours of rest during the cycle of rotation: thus in a three-week cycle including 120 hours off at times when shifts change over, the normal direction of rotation (morning, afternoon, night) gives successively two weekly rest periods of 48 hours and one of 24, while the opposite direction (night, afternoon, morning) gives, in succession, two weekly rest periods of 32 hours and one of 56. In certain cases this may have the effect of making the weekly rest period coincide with the weekend.

Length of Cycle of Rotation

This is the period necessary for an individual worker to come
back to the same sequence of days of work and rest over a number of
weeks. This length may vary from three to twenty weeks, at least
in the systems most commonly used. It is determined, in part, by the
number of crews required under the system adopted.

Hours of Weekly Rest and
Their Distribution

As already pointed out, the frequency and direction of rotation
determine the length of the weekly rest periods and their distribution
over the days of the week. Thus, these factors in combination can
lead to a variation in the length of the weekly rest period from
24 to 72 consecutive hours in the same cycle.

Number of Free Sundays

Depending on the system adopted and the length of the cycle, the
number of free Sundays will vary, so that there will be either one
free Sunday every four weeks or three free Sundays every nine weeks.
In certain cases a Sunday may go with a Saturday, giving a free
weekend, but this cannot happen more than once at most during any
given cycle of rotation.

Number of Crews, and
Related Variations

Since we are dealing with a three-shift system, it may appear at
first sight, that all that is necessary for the operation of such a
system is to divide the workers up into three crews. This was, in
fact, the arrangement most commonly used when the system was first
adopted. It had the serious disadvantage, however, of requiring one
of the crews to work a double shift at the end of the week so as to
facilitate the rotation of the crews on each particular shift (morning,
afternoon and night) and to enable the other two crews to have a
continuous rest period of 24 hours. Other systems have gradually
been developed to overcome this difficulty, as well as to reduce the
average number of hours worked per week (originally 56) and to increase
the number of rest days in the week. The use of a fourth crew is now
widespread, but other systems, as will be seen later, call for seven
crews or more.

The introduction of a fourth crew provides the basis for what
has sometimes been called the "rotating week". This system enables
one crew to rest while the other three are working; as a result, if
account is taken of the rotation of the crews among the three shifts
(morning, afternoon and night), rest days are spaced out over the
week. Thus, for a four-week cycle, one crew will be able to rest on
Monday and Tuesday in the first week, on Wednesday and Thursday in
the second, on Friday and Saturday in the third and on Sunday and
Monday in the fourth. Each crew is thus certain to have one Sunday
free during the cycle of rotation.

It should be noted that systems giving an average working week
of 42 hours - systems (1) and (2) below - have the advantage that
each crew has the same number of workers throughout. More complex
systems sometimes make it necessary to bring additional workers into
the crews to enable them to operate.

It should also be pointed out that the length of the cycle of
rotation can be varied by changing the frequency of rotation; if
crews change over every six days, the length of the cycle is 24 weeks;
if the change takes place every five days, the length of the cycle
is 20 weeks; if every four days, 16 weeks; if every three days,
12 weeks; and if every two days, 8 weeks.

As the frequency of rotation decreases, the length of the rest
periods after the crews change over tends to decrease, those rest
periods themselves then being more frequent.

In the systems most commonly used, with changeovers every four
or five days, it is possible to make the longest rest periods coincide
with the end of the night shift, which is generally considered to be
the most tiring.

A number of systems are described below[1]; it should be noted
that, in the tables, the four crews are designated by the letters a,
b, c and d.

(1) Four-crew system with a four-week cycle of rotation. Crews
change over every seven days in the four-week cycle, two rotations
being followed by rest periods of 48 hours each while the third
rotation is followed by a rest period of 72 hours, including Sunday.
The average length of the working week is then 42 hours.

Assignment	1st week MTWTFSS	2nd week MTWTFSS	3rd week MTWTFSS	4th week MTWTFSS
Morning shift	aaaaaaa	bbbbbbb	ccccccc	ddddddd
Afternoon shift	ccddddd	ddaaaaa	aabbbbb	bbccccc
Night shift	bbbbccc	ccccddd	ddddaaa	aaaabbb
Day off	ddccbbb	aaddccc	bbaaddd	ccbbaaa

(2) Four-crew system with a 20-week cycle of rotation. Here
again, the average length of the working week is 42 hours. Crews
change over every five days. The rest periods following the changes
are of 48 or 72 hours. Each crew has five free Sundays over the
total cycle of rotation.

Assignment	1st week MTWTFSS	2nd week MTWTFSS	3rd week MTWTFSS	4th week MTWTFSS
Morning shift	aaaaabb	bbbcccc	cddddda	aaaabbb
Afternoon shift	ccddddd	aaaaabb	bbbcccc	cddddda
Night shift	bbbcccc	cddddda	aaaabbb	bbccccc
Day off	ddcbbaa	dccbbad	dccbaad	dcbbaad etc.

---

[1] Others are described in appendix 3.

If a system in which crews change over every six days is
adopted, this gives a 24-week cycle of rotation.

(3) <u>Four-crew system with irregular frequency of rotation</u>.
The systems so far described have constant frequencies of rotation,
every seven, six, five or four days, but others have varying frequencies,
as in the case of what is sometimes called the "Continental" system.
Under that system crews change over sometimes after two days and
sometimes after three, the rest periods being also of either two or
three days.

The system most commonly used has a 28-day cycle of rotation:

Assignment	1st week MTWTFSS	2nd week MTWTFSS	3rd week MTWTFSS	4th week MTWTFSS
Morning shift	aaddccb	bbaaddc	ccbbaad	ddccbba
Afternoon shift	bbaaddc	ccbbaad	ddccbba	aaddccb
Night shift	ccbbaad	ddccbba	aaddccb	bbaaddc
Day off	ddccbba	aaddccb	bbaaddc	ccbbaad

It will be noticed here that the three consecutive rest days that
occur once in the cycle for each crew coincide with a weekend;   there
are two free Sundays every 8 weeks.

A variation on the system just described is that with rotation
every two days, which gives an 8-week cycle. The rest periods are all
of 48 hours and also include two Sundays during the cycle. It should
be noted, however, that if a backward shift rotation is introduced
(each crew moves from the afternoon shift to the morning shift, and
so on), a rest period of 56 hours is obtained when the crews change
over from the night shift to the earlier shift.

(4) <u>Mixed systems</u>. Among the possible variations on the systems
described above, the system with seven half-crews is of particular
interest. This system is so called because each shift (morning,
afternoon and night) is worked by two half-crews, each of which has
its own rotation schedule. As a result there are six half-crews
working in every period of 24 hours, while one half-crew is resting;
hence the reference to seven half-crews. The cycle is seven weeks
in length, divided up into 42 working days and seven rest days.

The following is an example of this system (the seven half-
crews are designated by the letters a, b, c, d, e, f and g).

Assignment	1st week MTWTFSS	2nd week MTWTFSS	3rd week MTWTFSS	4th week MTWTFSS
Morning shift	aaaaaaa dddbbbb	ggggggg bbbeeee	fffffff eeecccc	ddddddd cccaaaa
Afternoon shift	ecccccc ffffddd	caaaaaa ddddbbb	aggggggg bbbbeee	gffffff eeecccc
Night shift	bbeeeee ggggggff	eecccccc fffffddd	ccaaaaa dddddbb	aaggggg bbbbbee
Day off	cebdfgg	acebdff	gacebdd	fgacebb etc.

It will be seen that for a given crew the end of an assignment to one shift is separated from the beginning of an assignment to another by 24 hours, except in the case of rotation from the night shift to the morning shift, where the gap is 48 hours.   There is one free Saturday and Sunday every seven weeks in this cycle.

Other variations exist, for example that whereby normal working days are introduced among the days on shift work.   These days, known as "relay" days, generally follow a rest day, and are worked by the fourth crew, while the three others work the shifts (morning, afternoon and night).   This system may meet the special needs of the organisation of work in certain industries.[1]

Determining Factors

The examples quoted are intended only as an illustration of the wide range of shift systems that exist.   The advantages and drawbacks of the main systems will be considered in the next two chapters.

It should be emphasised at this stage, however, that the adoption of these systems in undertakings does not always appear to be essential from the point of view of organisation, or to be technically or economically necessary.   Most commonly, the use of a particular system is the consequence of local or industrial custom; when several systems coexist in the same industry, or in the same undertaking, this is sometimes solely as a result of the action of a particular individual, whether a manager, an engineer or a shop foreman.   At best, the preferences of the workers may have been taken into account, but it is rare for the adoption of a particular system to be the result of a study not only of the technical, economic and organisational factors involved but also of all the individual and social needs of the workers.   Yet it will be seen that the latter constitute, nevertheless, a major problem, if it is borne in mind that the adoption of a shift system is not merely the expression of technical and economic requirements but also affects individual, family and community life.

New systems may be developed as a result of a reduction in the hours of work;   this is, in fact, one of the factors encouraging such innovation.   Thus, a reduction in the hours of work has made it possible, with the use of a fourth crew, to change from a three-shift system, with an average of 56 hours a week, to the system now most commonly used with an average working week of 42 hours.

Since the reduction of hours of work has encouraged (and is still encouraging) the extension of shift work, it may also be thought that it will lead to an improvement in its organisation that will be to the advantage of the workers and, as a consequence, of society as a whole.

------

[1] This system, together with that of the seven half-crews, has been adopted in the iron and steel industry.

CHAPTER IV

EFFECTS ON THE WORKER'S PERFORMANCE AND HEALTH

Shift work is not just a device which management can use to
increase the productivity of an undertaking. It dictates a chronological pattern of living that directly affects the behaviour of
the worker both at work and in his family and social life. It is
not surprising that the earliest studies on shift work were concerned with its effects on the worker's health, since the rhythms
imposed by this method of working are obviously in conflict with
those governing the major biological functions of nutrition and
sleep. Although the many studies carried out in this field have
sometimes yielded contradictory results, owing in most cases to
methodological difficulties, a consensus is gradually emerging on
certain points, and provides the elements of a pathology of shift
work or, more generally, a pathology of changing work schedules.

The effects of shift work on the worker's health were investigated before its repercussions on family and social life because
shift work was adopted for economic reasons. It was necessary to
measure the effects of shift work on all the factors of production,
and the worker was regarded as such a factor. The study of labour
output, industrial accidents or absenteeism thus necessarily
involved the study of the pathological effects of this way of
organising the work.

It will be seen, however, that the harmfulness of shift work
has been highlighted by much research not concerned with the economic aspects; such research pointed the way to preventive selection
procedures and to vocational rehabilitation, and also provided a
stimulus to restrict the use of this method of working and to
improve its organisation.

A separate discussion of the effects of shift work on behaviour
at work, on health and on social life respectively is clearly
based on an arbitrary division of the subject, since most studies
stress the interdependence of the physiological, psychological and
social factors involved. An interdisciplinary approach is therefore required. Before the interaction of those factors is demonstrated, however, it is important to identify them. The present
chapter therefore deals with the effects of shift work on the
behaviour of the worker in the undertaking (output, safety and
absenteeism) and on his physiological functions, while the repercussions of this method of working on the workers' family and
social life will be analysed in greater detail in the next chapter.

Work Performance

While the First World War encouraged the extension of shift
work, especially in the armaments industry[1], it also gave rise,
particularly in the United Kingdom and the United States, to a
large number of investigations into the physiological effects of

---

[1] Shift work made it possible to increase productivity and to
make the best possible use of the female labour available.

recurring changes in hours of work, and thus into the repercussions
of shift work on various aspects of the worker's performance.

Output and Productivity

The question first studied was that of the effects of shift
work on the worker's output and productivity. Such an investigation was found to present a number of difficulties. A comparison
of the output of workers on shift work with that of workers on a
normal routine gives rise to certain methodological difficulties,
since in most cases two different populations are involved: this
is the result not only of the selection process when the workers
are engaged but also of a self-selection process by the workers
themselves. Even if the study is carried out in the same branch
of economic activity, or even in a single undertaking, the work
done will rarely be comparable, not only because of the content of
the job, but above all because of the conditions under which it is
performed in the different cases. It is therefore necessary to
compare different shifts (morning, afternoon and night) within a
given system of shift rotation, or in other words, to study the
differences in output between shifts, account also being taken of
the position of each shift within the cycle of rotation. Hypotheses that may be tested are, for example, that the output of
the night shift will be smaller than that of the morning shift or
the afternoon shift, or that the output of the night shift will
decrease as the time for the changeover approaches.

Theories on this subject are based on two types of explanation.[1]
Certain authors believe that the output of the night shift should
be smaller than that of the day shifts because physiological
rhythms should reduce working capacity at night. Other writers
place greater stress on external factors, and in particular on the
smaller number of supervisory personnel, the lack of over-all co-
ordination of production, and the inadequacy of the technical
assistance available at night.

Several surveys have been carried out on this subject, or
have been concerned explicitly with this problem. No attempt will
be made to give a comprehensive review of them; all that is necessary here is to describe the most striking results, while at the
same time pointing out the difficulty of reaching conclusions that
are final or capable of general application.

As early as 1924 Farmer, in a survey carried out in the glass
industry in the United Kingdom, found that the highest output was
obtained by the afternoon shift and the lowest by the morning
shift.[2] A report published in the United States in 1927 for the
National Industrial Conference Board (New York) showed that, based
on information supplied by some 250 companies employing more than
a million persons, the output of workers on the night shift was
qualitatively and quantitatively below that of workers of the day
shifts, although the difference was not very great. The same

---

[1] See Kabaj: "Shift work and employment expansion: towards
an optimum pattern", op. cit., p. 251 et seq.

[2] The complete list of references to this chapter is given in
Part III of appendix 5.

report also stressed the effect of the way in which the shifts were organised. During the First World War, a period in which there was a considerable incentive to extend shift work, numerous surveys, both in the United States and in the United Kingdom, were conducted in an attempt to find an answer to this question. Although certain differences in output, to the disadvantage of the night shift, were noted, they were not of decisive importance. In the same way, in the USSR, at the beginning of the first five-year plan, some studies showed that "the output of the night shift would appear to be only between 4.5 and 6 per cent less than that of the morning and day shifts respectively".[1]

More precise information has been provided, however, by more recent and more systematic surveys. That carried out by Wyatt and Marriot in 1945-46 in a metallurgical undertaking may be mentioned first. They studied a group of workers organised into two shifts, namely a day shift and a night shift, and found that the average hourly output was higher on the day shift, irrespective of the frequency of rotation (weekly, fortnightly, or monthly). They emphasise, however, that the number of hours worked per day is smaller for the night shifts; that output on Saturday morning, the lowest of the week, was not included in their calculations; and that since the night shift workers were paid higher wages, it was possible that they were adjusting their output in relation to the weekly wage that they wished to earn. Comparing the results of their inquiry on rates of output with the views of the workers concerned, they noted that 68 per cent preferred day work, and they concluded that, as night work required an additional effort in order to achieve results similar to those obtained on the day shifts, the differences found could be attributed to the fatigue inherent in night work. When, however, they continued their survey on a group of workers who changed shift every fortnight, they found that the hourly rates of output were higher during the second week, for both day shifts and night shifts. This would seem to be an effect of habituation, which will be considered again later. Nevertheless, these authors also point out that a third of the workers worked as well or even better on night work; this emphasises the importance of personal factors which could be taken into consideration when the workers are selected.

Another survey was carried out in Poland in 1965 by the Institute for Social Studies. The survey was conducted in nine factories belonging to five branches of industry, and covered the output rate of about 18,360 man-days worked in three shifts over a period of three months. The results of this inquiry are very similar to those obtained by Wyatt and Marriott.[2] On average, the highest output was achieved during the afternoon shift and the lowest during the night shift, though the differences were fairly small.

---

[1] "The seven-hour day in Soviet Russia", *International Labour Review*, Vol. XXII, No. 3, September 1930, p. 349. See also P. M. Dubner and I. L. Kremlev: *24 chasa v sutki* (Moscow, 1931), pp. 55-72.

[2] See Kabaj: "Shift work and employment expansion: towards an optimum pattern", op. cit., pp. 253-254. The results of these surveys are summarised in two tables.

Vernon had already shown in 1943, however, that permanent
night work leads to a decrease in output which, as compared with
day work, may amount to as much as 17 per cent.   To the extent
that the reduction in output may be considered as an index of
harmfulness, it would therefore seem that permanent night work is
not preferable to a rotating routine.

Such results must nevertheless be interpreted with a good deal
of caution.   Thus, many authors have emphasised the repercussions
of the total number of hours worked on output, irrespective of the
shift worked.   Vernon, in a survey conducted in 1939, showed that
output increases if the number of hours worked per shift is reduced
from ten to eight.   Kossoris made the same finding.

Andlauer and Fourre, in their bibliographical survey of the
ergonomic aspects of rotating shift work, emphasised the limitations of the research carried out so far and the need to make
additional experimental studies in order to obtain more precise
results.   It is clear, in fact, that it is difficult to carry out
research in factories since working conditions vary too greatly.
Moreover the nature of the work and the skills of the workers are
often different as between ordinary day work and shift working
round the clock.   The same doubts have been expressed by Ulich, who
correctly pointed out that workers often feel that their output is
much lower at night, whereas in reality they are working under
greater difficulties.

Errors and Accidents

The study of the effects of work schedules on industrial accidents is linked with that of effects on the occurrence of errors
at work, since most frequently an accident is the consequence of an
error.   A large number of inquiries have been conducted on this
subject.

Kleitman showed that a close correlation existed between the
central temperature and intellectual performance.   The research
of greatest relevance, however, in this connection is that of
Bjerner, Holm and Swensson (1955) on the mistakes made in the
recording of meter readings in a gas works in Sweden.   A three-
shift system was being worked, with a weekly rotation.   The study
covered readings made between 1912 and 1931;   75,000 mistakes were
made in the course of 175,000 recordings.   The curve of error
variation derived from these data showed a circadian type of variation, with a peak at 3 a.m. and another around 3 p.m.;   a fall was
observed between 5 and 7 a.m.   A reduction in the hours of work
(from 56 to 48 per week) failed to change the shape of the curve.
This has been confirmed by other investigations.

In fact, however, the link between the incidence of errors at
work and the industrial accident rate is not as close as might be
imagined.   Although certain studies have shown a steady increase in
the frequency of accidents during the day, Vernon, investigating
for the first time the frequency of accidents on the night shift,
found a steady decrease in this frequency from the beginning to the
end of the shift.   It may be supposed, therefore, that the mech-
anism underlying the occurrence of accidents is different for day
work and night work.

The study carried out at the applied physiology laboratory of the Faculty of Medicine of Strasbourg University by F. Andlauer and B. Metz calls for mention here, since it has provided the basis for new theories concerning the frequency and seriousness of accidents occurring on night shifts. The study, initially conducted in a metallurgical plant, was concerned with industrial accidents among workers operating a three-shift system. The results are shown below, namely the distribution over the three shifts of the number of workers (expressed as the total number of hours of work), the output (in tons of the various products) and the number of accidents, as a percentage of the total for 1949.

Item	Shifts			
	Morning	Evening	Night	All
Number of workers	33.45	33.31	33.22	100.00
Output	33.07	34.09	32.82	100.00
Accidents	36.21	37.99	25.79	100.00

The number of workers was the same on the three shifts, so that the proportion expected was 33.3 per cent. As far as output is concerned, it will be seen that the differences are small, although the results of the inquiries previously presented are confirmed. By contrast a marked difference can be seen, in respect of the frequency of accidents, between the night shift and the other shifts. These results have been confirmed by those of other studies carried out by the same authors on the statistical data for 11,000 accidents. When they considered the seriousness of the accidents, however, they found a serious accident rate of 32.5 per cent for the morning and evening shifts and one of 35 per cent for the night shift. During the day, therefore, accidents are more frequent but less serious, while at night they are less frequent but more serious. The authors conclude by putting forward the following hypothesis: during the night, because of the depression of higher nervous activity, mental disturbances capable of upsetting acquired occupational habits would appear to play a smaller part than during the day. Since such disturbances play an important role in the aetiology of industrial accidents, the latter are less frequent during the night. Conversely, when reactions are inhibited, accidents would be less frequent but more serious.[1]

It must therefore be concluded that, although research in this field has yielded interesting results, these are by no means definitive at the present time, so that other investigations are necessary.

Absenteeism

Absenteeism is a favourite field of analysis in the study of labour problems. Like accident rates and output, it provides a means of assessing the degree of adjustment to shift work, and many authors have used absenteeism as a criterion of harmfulness.

---

[1] P. Andlauer and L. Fourre: Aspects ergonomiques du travail en équipes alternantes (Strasbourg, Centre d'études de physiologie appliquée au travail, 1962), p. 26.

Brusgaard, on the basis of a survey conducted in Norway,
thought that absenteeism rates were higher among shift workers than
among workers on normal work schedules. The majority of authors,
however, emphasise that absenteeism is mainly dependent on the
length of the working day, and that above a certain number of
hours absenteeism increases to much the same extent for both day
work and night work.

Wyatt and Marriott, in the survey already mentioned, showed
that absenteeism was lower for the night shift than for the day
shift, but that during a four-week cycle of rotation the frequency
of absences tended to increase for the night shift and to decrease
for the day shift. It may be thought that the fatigue accumulated
during the night shift might have an effect on the first few weeks
of work on the day shift. Other explanations can be put forward,
namely, the tendency of the shift worker to take on additional work
("double jobbing") when he is on day work, or the fact that wages
are higher on the night shift.

The results obtained from the survey conducted in the
Scandinavian countries by Thiis-Evensen from 1947 to 1956 covering
2,885 workers on day work and 3,263 workers on shift work confirmed
those obtained by Wyatt and Marriott: the rate of absenteeism was
higher among day workers, but if those transferred were excluded,
absenteeism was about the same for the two categories of workers.
Aanonsen, who studied absenteeism from the pathological point of
view, arrived at similar results.

Thus, the information available does not seem to indicate
any particular effect of shift work on absenteeism, at least as far
as long periods of absence are concerned. It should be noted,
however, that an investigation dealing solely with workers operating a system of two 8-hour shifts with shift rotation on the one
hand and permanent shifts on the other showed that absenteeism was
higher in the first case.

If the various shifts under a three-shift system are compared,
a tendency will be noted for the rate of absenteeism to be higher
for the night shift, and for it to increase over the weeks in the
case of a long cycle of rotation (every four weeks, for example).
This brings us back to the point of view of psychologists, who
regard absenteeism as a sign of lack of adaptation to work: "the
indecisive attitude of someone who cannot make up his mind either
to stay or to go", as Jardiller has put it.

It is striking, however, that although they have not been able
to demonstrate the validity of their view in this respect, the
authors of most of the studies on this subject have emphasised the
importance of psychological and sociological factors, which act in
conjunction with the work schedules. It would be desirable for
this aspect of the problem to be the subject of future research.

A final point to be borne in mind in this connection is that
the studies carried out so far have by no means produced final conclusions with regard to the effect of shift work whether on output,
accidents or absenteeism. They are of interest, nevertheless,
because they have demonstrated the complexity of the problems
involved and the interdependence of physiological and sociological
factors. Many investigations carried out purely from a physiological or medical point of view suffer, in fact, from an inability
to grasp labour problems, which cannot be encompassed by simple

measurements of output, errors or absences; the effects of living
conditions (housing, distance between work and home) and of ways of
life on work are too often ignored.

Physiological Aspects

Of the studies on shift work, those concerned with the
physiological and medical aspects are among the most numerous.
These studies have been mainly concerned with two different purposes -
the demonstration of the harmfulness, if any, of shift work, and the
search for characteristic psycho-pathological or physio-pathological
reactions to this method of working.[1]

To attempt to sum up the results of these studies would be to
go beyond the scope of this publication, the object of which is
rather to indicate the perspectives opened up by the work done so
far. Even if the results are far from being conclusive their
general trend will help to draw attention to certain aspects of the
harmfulness of shift work and to the contra-indications to such
work.

Before the main aspects of the pathology of shift work can be
presented, however, it is necessary to emphasise the nature and
characteristics of the circadian or nyctohemeral rhythm, as seen
in man. This rhythm, whose main feature is the alternation of day
and night, is, of course, not limited to man; it is found in most
living beings, whether plants or animals. Nevertheless, in man,
this rhythm has complex effects on the whole range of bodily and
mental functions.

As far as shift work is concerned, the circadian rhythm must
be considered, on the one hand, from the point of view of the
functions that it affects, and on the other, from the point of view
of its permanence, so that the possibilities and conditions for its
displacement in time or its inversion can be assessed.

The majority of biological rhythms are linked to the circadian
rhythm. Thus it is known that cardiac rhythms slow down during
sleep. Arterial pressure undergoes similar variations, going through
a maximum in the middle of the day and a minimum in the middle of
the night, around 2 a.m. When a person works at night, his
cardiovascular function is depressed in the same way, but to a
smaller extent than during sleep; in addition, the warmer the
surroundings in which the person works, the slighter the degree of
the depression. Changes in respiratory function are on the same
scale, and the same applies to the digestive (gastric and hepatic)
secretions.

The central temperature is generally used as an index of the
circadian rhythm. Some research, particularly by Metz and Sigwalt,
has shown that the difference between the resting and working
central temperatures, in the absence of heat load, is the same for
the three shifts (morning, afternoon and night) and that the

---

[1] Andlauer and Fourre, op cit., p. 39.

variations are also similar, with a minimum at 4 a.m. (the rhythm of the central temperature does not entirely coincide with that of the biological functions).

The problem of the inversion of this rhythm has been the main point at issue in discussions on the worker's adjustment to shift rotation. The studies of Kleitman on the crews of submarines, those of the National Aeronautics and Space Administration of the United States on astronauts, the investigations carried out in France on the basis of extended periods spent in underground caves, in particular by Siffre, have provided (and will continue to provide) a great deal of information on the ability of individuals to invert their rhythm and to adapt to rhythms other than the waking-sleeping rhythm of 24 hours.

Several studies have shown that certain individuals can invert their circadian rhythm after two or three days, while others need nearly a week and in certain cases inversion is impossible.

The possibility of inversion (or at least of reducing the amplitude of the curve) is obviously one of the main criteria of adjustment to rotating work schedules. In fact, the majority of studies, in particular those of Bonjer in the Netherlands, have shown that in most cases the individual's adjustment to shift rotation is only partial. A certain distortion of the circadian rhythm persists, with a raised minimum in the morning and a reduced maximum in the evening. In addition, a return to normal hours of work leads to the restoration of the normal circadian rhythm (see also Andlauer and Metz).

What are, however, the pathological effects of shift work, in view of the marked stability of certain physiological rhythms? The harmfulness of the system may find expression in various disorders, particularly digestive or cardiac malfunctions, nervous symptoms, and sleep disturbances.

Of the various manifestations of the harmfulness of shift work, two call for particular attention: digestive disorders, which are the most commonly mentioned, and sleep disturbances.[1]

Digestive Disorders

Digestive disorders are of many types, and a distinction may be made between gastric or duodenal ulcers and the whole range of dyspeptic disorders. Of the large number of studies carried out in this field, one of the most important is that of Aanonsen, in Norway, who investigated, at the same time, day workers, workers on the three-shift system then in use, and workers who had been taken off shift work. The results of this inquiry, shown in the following table, demonstrate that only workers who had been transferred because of their inability to tolerate shift work had suffered any damage to their health. In contrast, the incidence of pathological conditions was not greater among those still working under the three-shift system than among those who had always worked normal hours.

---

[1] Only the most important disorders will be considered here; specialised studies, listed in the bibliography, deal with minor disorders such as lack of appetite or intestinal disorders.

Frequency of observed disorders, among 350 workers,
expressed as a percentage of the number of workers
in each category

Nature of disorders	Day workers	Workers on three-shift system	Workers formerly on three-shift system
Gastric disorders	7.5	6.0	19.0
Ulcers	6.6	10.0	32.5
Intestinal disorders	11.6	10.2	10.6
Nervous complaints	13.0	10.0	32.5
Cardiovascular disorders	2.6	1.1	0.9

Source: A. Aanonsen: "Medical problems of shift work", in
Industrial Medicine and Surgery (Oslo), No. 28, 1959,
pp. 422-427.

As far as the incidence of gastric ulcers, in particular, is
concerned, this question has been studied by a large number of
authors, but the results are often contradictory. Workers transferred from the three-shift system should be considered separately,
as was done by Aanonsen. In addition, the confirmation of the
existence of an ulcer, as pointed out by Hadengne, is based on a
difficult diagnosis; its origins are complex, and many physiologists
stress, among other things, the effect of psychosomatic factors.

Many authors have emphasised the importance of working conditions and eating habits. It may be pointed out, in this connection,
that comparative studies should take into account the eating habits
typical of different countries, since meal times and the food eaten
may vary with the local culture.

Sleep Disturbances

Sleep disturbances occupy a special place in the pathology of
shift work where night work is involved. They are clearly one of
the inevitable consequences of this method of working, and the
majority of authors consider them responsible, in turn, for the
whole range of nervous disorders.

Thus Thiis-Evensen, in an inquiry conducted in Denmark and
already mentioned, showed that 60 per cent of shift workers, as
compared with 11 per cent of day workers, suffered from sleep
disturbances. He added that the inability to make good the fatigue
associated with a succession of night shifts results in an accumulation of fatigue, with a disastrous effect on the sympathetic
nervous system.

Analysing in greater detail the cause of sleep disturbances,
on the basis of an inquiry among workers, he indicated that one of
the main causes is noise: street traffic, factory noises, domestic
noises. Housing conditions are clearly responsible to a large
extent for this state of affairs. Shift workers complain about them
much more often than do workers on normal day work.

The duration of sleep, in addition, is too short for the majority of shift workers on rotating systems, and sleep disturbances occur more frequently among them than among those who are permanently on night work. Only a few studies, however, have taken account so far of the effects of the frequency of rotation on sleep disturbances. Physiologists generally conclude from the results of their research that permanent night work or systems with long cycles of rotation should be preferable to a weekly shift rotation, which is often incorrectly considered to be normal industrial practice, whereas it is only a collection of habits and customs whose permanance is most often the result only of inertia or resistance to change. The hypothesis that a long cycle of rotation (of as long as a month, for example) would enable individuals to adapt better to the inversion of the circadian rhythm has not been confirmed, however, by several recent inquiries, carried out particularly in the United Kingdom and in France; on the contrary, these studies emphasise the advantages of rapidly rotating patterns, with rotation every two or three days.

Thus Murrel stated that workers on a rapidly rotating rota (every two days) had less sickness. Of course, it cannot be concluded from workers' preference for rapidly rotating patterns (see De La Mare, Walker and Wedderburn) that workers employed under such patterns no longer have any physiological problems. Nevertheless, although the main objections to rapid rotation so far put forward were based on the need for a complete inversion of the circadian rhythm, authors such as Van Loon and Wilkinson have raised certain doubts in that connection. It is not impossible that changes of shift at short intervals may rapidly develop new rhythms of reduced amplitude (see Lobban and Tredre).

No conclusion can yet be reached on this subject, and premature commitment to what are often wrongly believed to be fixed and immutable truths should be avoided. It is important to realise that there is scope for further research on this matter. All the experts agree that many of the functions and requirements of the various kinds of sleep are still unknown.

Other inquiries have shown that the duration of sleep varies, depending on whether the worker is on the morning, evening or night shift. Thus Caillot has found that 38.5 per cent of workers on the night shift sleep at least 8 hours, while the figures are 46 per cent for workers on the afternoon shift and 93 per cent for those on the morning shift. These results, whose general trend was confirmed by the inquiry conducted by M. Maurice and C. Monteil[1], show the existence of a kind of recuperation among workers on the afternoon shift, but this recuperation is possible only every three weeks; there is therefore an accumulation of fatigue during the cycle of rotation of the three-shift system. This is confirmed by the workers themselves, when they are asked. They feel more tired when they work on the night and morning shifts, which often leads them to prefer the afternoon shift.

---

[1] Vie quotidienne et horaires de travail, Enquête psycho-sociologique sur le travail en équipes successives (Paris, Université, Institut des sciences sociales du travail, 1965).

Conclusions

No definite conclusions can be reached on the basis of the studies whose main results have been described above, although there seems to be a certain consensus with regard to a number of points. Additional and more systematic research is needed in this field so that further information can be obtained; the scattered nature of the research carried out so far and the failure of the results obtained to yield a coherent picture are factors that hinder the progress of the research. Long-term studies whereby the specific effects of certain factors could be monitored and cause-and-effect relationships established would also be of great value.

A number of studies have shown that the disorders associated with shift work are of psychosomatic origin and are linked with pathological states of the sympathetic nervous system. Castelnuovo-Tedesco concluded his study of persons suffering from gastric ulcers by stating that these were often individuals "trapped" in a situation in which they felt themselves to be helpless and on the verge of defeat. Is this not precisely the situation of certain workers for whom the only alternatives are shift work or unemployment (or at best a marked decrease in earnings[1]), and whose ability to adapt physiologically to changes in living patterns is low? They may not be suffering from ulcers, perhaps, but from a whole range of disorders (sleep disturbances, digestive disorders, irritability, etc.) that gradually render their state of health increasingly critical. The psychosomatic approach does not seem to have been sufficiently widely used in the study of the pathology of shift work.

In contrast, many studies have stressed the effect of such factors as working and housing conditions, job interest, family relations and integration in the local community, on various pathological disorders. Nevertheless, these factors, even if they are mentioned, are rarely taken into account in the working hypotheses and are not used in the interpretation of the results.

For this reason, co-operation between doctors, physiologists, psychologists, psychiatrists and sociologists would seem to be necessary in order to promote interdisciplinary research; but it is important to be aware, from the start, of the methodological and epistemological problems that such an approach involves, if the "parallel dilettantism" denounced by P. F. Lazarsfeld[2] is to be avoided.

One point on which agreement has been reached is that the harmfulness of shift work is due essentially to the disturbance of physiological functions that are linked to rhythmical patterns. Physiologists have been able to identify a large number of rhythms, which are in addition interdependent, and it is agreed that the ability to adjust to new rhythms varies widely from one individual to another, while external factors may also play a part. While such rhythms have been acquired as a response to the environment in

---

[1] It is not always possible to transfer a worker to another job in an undertaking operating a three-shift system, and if it is possible, the worker must often accept a fairly marked drop in earnings.

[2] In M. Komarovsky (ed.): Common frontiers of the social sciences (New York, Free Press, 1957).

the course of the long history of human evolution, there are no
doubt situations in which it is desirable for men to adjust rapidly
to a new environment. Shift work may be one of these situations,
but since it has been created by industrial society in order to meet
certain technical and economic requirements, it may also be asked to
what extent man should adapt himself to a state of affairs that
disturbs, in particular, his fundamental physiological rhythms, and
whether it would not be better to change certain aspects of the
situation, at the risk of reducing the productivity of the undertaking. This fundamental question will be raised on several
occasions in this study. The answer will doubtless not be clear
cut, since solutions can be found that are compatible with the
rhythm of bodily functions[1], at least if technical and operational
research are used in the service of man and society and not exclusively in that of special economic interests.

---

[1] Suggestions will be made, in this connection, in subsequent
chapters and in the general conclusions of the study. It is probable
that no general solution will be found, but only solutions valid for
a particular undertaking or type of industry.

CHAPTER V

EFFECTS ON FAMILY AND SOCIAL LIFE

Shift work is often contrasted with "normal" day work, and those who work under a system of two or three 8-hour shifts generally consider that they are not leading a normal existence, that their life is "different", etc. This is clearly one of the main accusations made against this method of working. It is therefore surprising that so little scientific research has been carried out on this aspect of shift work, particularly when many social groups, such as the trade unions, the employers and even the churches, have taken up a stand on it, some denouncing shift work and others claiming that it is not so harmful. It is unfortunate that psychologists and sociologists have not shown the same interest as physicians and physiologists in the study of shift work, which the latter see almost as an experimental situation for the investigation of changes in biological rhythms; from the point of view of the social sciences, shift work is a field of the greatest interest for research, particularly on the interactions between life at work and life outside it, or in connection with an economic analysis of costs and benefits.

The main question is why the shift worker lives "on the margin" of society, and the meaning of the expressions, such as "different", "out of step" or "abnormal", often used by the shift worker to describe his way of life. The approach taken in this chapter is as follows: since shift work is defined by a certain time pattern, what are the effects of that pattern on family or social activities linked to other time patterns?

It is true that the main activities of industrial societies are organised around the "normal" working day; the majority of economic activities are carried out during the day, between 8 or 9 a.m. and 6 or 7 p.m. Although there is a fairly general tendency to extend the day by activities carried out in the evening, such activities still involve only a minority of workers and concern only a minority of users.

Patterns of work or of leisure, of hours of work and time off, are part of the organisation of every society and the more a society systematises its organisation and operation the more important predictability becomes; it is not by chance that certain sociologists regard post-industrial society as being essentially a "programmed" society. It is thus easier to understand the disadvantages, for both individuals and groups, of being subjected to work schedules that change every week, and sometimes even several times a week. Family life, in the first place, is greatly disturbed by such changes in rhythm, but so is social life, in the case of the most highly organised activities (entertainments, clubs and societies), as well as those which, while more informal or spontaneous in character, nevertheless occupy an important place in social life (visits to friends, visits to places where drinks are served, relations with neighbours, etc.).

The use of free time is thus governed by a pattern of various activities, some being fixtures and others more spontaneous and unplanned, but all giving time its social significance and value.

This conception of time is remote from that of the economist or
the efficiency expert for whom the only measure of time is its
cost, in line with the popular saying that time is money.

In considering, in succession, the effects of shift work on
the family and social life of the workers, reference will be made,
in support of the views expressed above, to the few studies
recently carried out in this field.

Family Life

A distinction will be drawn between two aspects of family
life, namely its domestic organisation and the relations among the
various members of the family. The aim is to show and to explain
why, and to what extent, the shift worker does not participate
fully in family life, and then to define the effects of this on the
other members of the family.

In industrial society, the organisation of domestic life is
very closely linked with the whole range of rhythms imposed by the
work done during the day. While there may be differences between
one country and another, or between one society and another, daily
rhythms are everywhere organised in relation to meals, work and
sleep. Weekly rhythms, in turn, are based on a succession of five
or six working days followed by one or two days of rest at the weekend, on Saturday and Sunday. In relation to the most commonly
adopted organisation of domestic life, at least in Western societies,
the shift worker has either to adapt himself as far as he can to the
habits of the family, by waking up, for example, during the day so
that he can take part in the midday meal, or to make his family
follow his own timetable, by changing, for example, the times of
certain meals; if he does neither, he is forced to live to some
extent independently of his family. Whatever the solution adopted
- which may vary from one week to another in the case of a system
of three 8-hour shifts - there are many difficulties, which may
even become worse when several members of the same family have
irregular hours of work.

This whole range of difficulties has been mentioned in several
studies. Thus O. Banks[1], who conducted an inquiry among the wives
of shift workers who had changed over from a semi-continuous to a
continuous system of three 8-hour shifts, stated that 22 per cent
had found it more difficult to prepare meals. This was particularly marked in the case of systems of three 8-hour shifts in
that Sunday was no longer a permanent feature of the organisation
of family life.

Similar results were obtained in the inquiry carried out by
H.G. Brown: the wives of shift workers complained of the same
difficulties. Although they generally preferred their husbands to
work on the morning shift, because this enabled them to do their
housework and look after the children normally (this was not the

---

[1] For the complete list of references to this chapter, see
appendix 5 (mostly part III).

case when their husbands were resting or sleeping in the morning),
they then had the problem of preparing their husbands' meals at a
later time.   Under a system of three 8-hour shifts the wives also
had to change the organisation of domestic life every week.

Ulich, in an inquiry conducted in the Federal Republic of
Germany among workers employed under a three-shift system, found
that 74 per cent of married men and 45 per cent of bachelors complained of the disturbances in their family life associated with
this method of working.   He stresses a number of aspects that are
of particular importance to the wives of men on shift work:
impossibility of meeting friends or neighbours in the evening,
difficulties in sexual relations, and difficulties in the organisation of family life and in keeping house.   There is a transition
here from the difficulties encountered in the organisation of
domestic life to those affecting family relationships themselves,
the former clearly having an influence on the latter.   These
difficulties may, in addition, be made worse by housing conditions,
the size of the family, and the distance between the home and the
place of work and the means of transport used.

The most difficult situation is that of families of average
size, with two or three small children and poorly housed.   Such a
situation creates conditions that interfere with the rest of both
the worker and the other members of the family, who live in a
disturbed atmosphere because of the disruption of family life.
Ulich recorded 60 per cent of complaints of this kind among workers
on a routine of three 8-hour shifts, and 60 per cent again for
permanent night workers, but only 15 per cent among workers on two-
day shifts.

The inquiry carried out by Caillot showed clearly the way in
which these difficulties became more acute in relation to housing
conditions and size of family: rest was difficult for the worker
in 55 per cent of cases where the family had only two rooms
(including the kitchen), in 41 per cent of cases where the family
had three rooms, in 27 per cent of cases where it had four rooms,
and 7.6 per cent of cases where it had five rooms.   Interference
with rest also increased with the number of children, since it was
found in 24 per cent of families with one child, 40 per cent of
families with two children and 50 per cent of those with five.
The same inquiry, which covered 91 families, showed that only three
of them did not appear to change their pattern of living while the
father was resting, while the remainder considered that this rest
was a nuisance to all the other members of the family.

Other research more directly centred on the effects of shift
work on family and social life has provided more detailed information on this subject.   Thus an inquiry conducted by M. Maurice and
C. Monteil in France in 1965 showed that only under systems of three
8-hour shifts husbands on the night shift could be present (in
45 per cent of cases) at the two main daily meals (i.e. the mid-day
and the evening meal) so that it can be assumed that he broke his
sleep in order to be present at the mid-day meal.   When they were
on the afternoon shift, more than a quarter of the workers did not
take any of their meals with the family.   The coming together of
the family at meal times appeared to occur much less regularly than
with normal day work;   this situation is becoming increasingly
common in large towns, particularly because of the short lunch break
now being adopted in large undertakings.   It should be noted,
however, that it is quite common, with a normal working day, for

the entire family not to meet for the mid-day meal. What is the situation with regard to the number of hours spent together by husband and wife during the day, in relation to the various types of work schedule? Workers employed under a three-shift system are present for a larger number of hours than those employed under a two-shift system or on normal day work, but this may vary from one shift to another as in the case of meals taken together. The morning shift and the night shift give a larger amount of time off; the extent to which husband and wife are together will depend, however, on the type of work done by the wife.

Meals taken together and time spent at home with the spouse were taken here as indices of the effects of shift work on the organisation of family life. Other questions, in the same inquiry, were designed to measure the constraints imposed on family life, and to define the difficulties of greatest importance.

Thus, 66 per cent of shift workers thought that there was a greater interference with their family life than in any other field, and the degree of interference felt increased in going from workers on a two-shift system (56 per cent) to workers on semi-continuous three-shift work (62 per cent), and finally to those on continuous three-shift work (75 per cent). In addition, it was found that the attitudes of the workers towards shift work and its methods of organisation were generally based on criteria associated with family life. Thus, of workers on continuous shift work, more than half thought that working on Sundays and public holidays was a "serious nuisance"; of these, 58 per cent gave family matters as the reason.

Mott, Mann, McLoughlin and Warwick approached this problem in a different way in their investigations of shift work. In studying the effects of shift work, in particular on family life, they analysed the different roles and obligations of the worker as a social being, and more particularly as a husband and father. At the conclusion of their analysis, the authors state that shift work is a factor that does interfere with the reciprocal roles of husband and wife, and with their role as parents. The sample covered by the inquiry included both workers permanently on after-noon and night shifts and workers on rotating shifts, and it was the latter who expressed the greatest dissatisfaction. The dissatisfaction was greater among workers who wished to change to another shift system. As has been found in several studies, workers on a system of three rotating 8-hour shifts seemed to suffer from the disadvantages of all the other systems. The complaints most frequently made by the workers or their wives relate to mutual support of husband and wife, relations with the children, opportunities for normal family life, and disturbances in marital relationships and sexual life. The authors carried their investigation still further, and studied the consequences of such a situation on role behaviour as a father, on family equili-brium and integration, and hence on marital happiness. Their conclusions may be formulated as follows: drawing a distinction between marital life and family integration, they consider that shift work affects these two concepts in two stages and at two levels. The conflict between work and the performance of certain marital or family roles is greater in the case of activities to which the various members of the family attach great importance. There also seems to be a cumulative effect of these difficulties or disturbances in the performance of the various roles (husband

and wife, father and mother, and so on), which leads to a reduction
in "marital happiness" and in the ability to co-ordinate family
activities and to minimise strain and friction among family members.
It should be noted that Wyatt and Marriott, in their inquiry of
1953, concluded that there were more divorces among shift workers.
Several authors have mentioned this possibility, and have stressed
the difficulty of a normal sex life and the way in which the wife
may be isolated during the night when the husband is working.   It
may also be asked, however, though this has not been confirmed,
whether certain workers whose marriage is already in difficulty
may not find a way of escape in this method of working.   The
psychosociological approach thus throws light on some of the
effects of shift work on family life, the family then being considered as a social subsystem, with its own system of roles and
role expectations.

     Most inquiries have arrived at conclusions that are more or
less similar: shift work, especially when it involves night work
or work on three rotating shifts, undoubtedly disturbs family
life, whether in relation to the organisation of domestic life,
relations within the family, marital relations or the role of the
father in the education of the children.   Although this last point
has been dealt with in only a small number of inquiries, that of
Mott, Mann, McLoughlin and Warwick constitutes an advance, thanks
to its approach to the various roles of the shift worker as
husband and father.

     It is necessary to stress here the importance of other factors
that may reduce or accentuate the repercussions of shift work on
family life: housing conditions, family size, the work done by the
wife and possibly also by the children, distance between home and
place of work, means of transport.   The work of P.H. Chombart
de Lauwe may be mentioned in this connection; he has given precise
examples of the disturbance of family life associated with the hours
of work of husband and wife.   When husband and wife are on
different shift-work rotas, situations develop that, although no
doubt relatively uncommon, demonstrate to the point of absurdity
the extent to which this method of working may disrupt social
relations within the family group.

Social Life

     A number of inquiries have stressed the effects of shift work
on social life, with regard both to relations with secondary groups
(neighbours, friends or people working in the same undertaking)
and to participation in more or less organised and institutionalised
social activities.   It may even be considered that the effects of
shift work in this respect are even more unavoidable than its
effects on family life.   In the case of the latter, in fact,
possible methods of adaptation or adjustment can be envisaged
(improvement of housing conditions, improved organisation of family
life), whereas in the case of social life, particularly organised
activities, such adjustment seems unlikely.   The German expression
"social death" is no doubt exaggerated, but it does reflect the
whole range of difficulties that markedly affect the worker's
social relationships.

These difficulties concern, in the first place, contacts with secondary groups (the extended family, friends, neighbours). The irregularity of the distribution of free time, which is the result of the irregularity of the work schedules, makes the continuity of such contacts more doubtful, even if they are not formal in character. This was demonstrated, for example, by two inquiries conducted by Floyd C. Mann for the Survey Research Center of the University of Michigan. Thus, Mann and Hoffmann studied, in two electric power stations, the effects of shift-work rotas on relations with friends and the family. In the older of the power stations, 48 per cent of the workers on normal day work stated that they saw their friends at least once a week, but the same situation was found with only 34 per cent of shift workers. In the newer power station, the same reply was given by 64 per cent of workers on normal day work and 41 per cent of those on shift work. It should be noted that, in this latter power station, changes in the work schedules had resulted in additional free time and days of rest. Blakelock, using the same question in an inquiry in a petroleum refinery, found, in this case, a smaller difference between the two categories of workers than in the power stations. The explanation for this difference, according to Mann, was to be found in the characteristics of the communities in which the inquiries were carried out: the power stations were located close to a large metropolitan area, while the refinery was in a small town. In the latter case, contacts were facilitated by the size of the community and by the fact that it was known as a shift-working town. Most of the industries, in fact, had adopted this method of working, so that it offered more opportunities for the workers to make contact with friends and enjoy recreational facilities, since the majority of the population followed the same pattern of living.

In their study of a printers' union, Lipsett, Trow and Coleman pointed out that night workers have more contacts with printers, who have the same work schedule as they do. Even if these contacts could be the result of other factors, such as similarity of interests, they did appear to be one method of coping with the restrictions on social life imposed by shift work.

The studies mentioned above showed no difference, or hardly any, between workers on normal day work and shift workers in respect of contacts with relatives. It would appear that shift work causes fewer difficulties in the field of contacts with the extended family than in that of contacts with friends, people in the same undertaking and neighbours. This has been confirmed by the research of Maurice and Monteil, and of Mott, Mann, McLoughlin and Warwick.

According to the results of an inquiry conducted in France, the extent of interference with contacts with friends increases in step with the constraints imposed by the work schedule: 10 per cent of workers on a two-shift system stated that interference with their contacts with friends was "very great" or "fairly great"; the corresponding figure for workers on a semi-continuous three-shift system was 29 per cent, and for workers on continuous shift work 48 per cent.

Other results have shown that workers on a three-shift system have a greater tendency, as compared with those on two-shift or normal day work, to have contacts with their colleagues at work.

It should be noted finally that, among those persons who found Sunday work to cause very great interference, 65 per cent thought that this also applied to the field of contacts with friends, Sunday being the preferred day for such contacts.

The inquiry conducted in the United States by Mott, Mann, McLoughlin and Warwick showed, in turn, that shift workers have greater difficulty, as compared with other workers, in making new friends and in participating in family gatherings or meetings with friends. This is felt most strongly by the youngest workers, and also by wives. In addition, workers on shift employed under rotating systems would appear to have fewer friends than other workers; this is particularly true of shift workers who are over 40 years old and who wish to change to another work schedule.

The more social life is linked with institutions and organisations, of course, the greater the difficulties tend to become, since most group activities are designed for those with "normal" hours of work, which are, in fact, those of most people. However, workers on a three-shift system are only rarely free in the evening; when they are on the night shift, they have to be at work at some time between 8 and 10 p.m. When they are on the afternoon shift, those are the times when they leave work. When they are on a continuous three-shift routine, they have only one Sunday free in four or seven while rest days during the week are irregularly distributed over the cycle of rotation. In addition, although in large towns or cities there is a wide range of leisure activities scattered throughout the week, even during the day, the situation is not the same in small towns, where leisure activities and entertainments are most commonly arranged at the weekend.

Several studies have shown the difficulties encountered by shift workers in their attempts to participate in group activities, such as taking part in the activities of clubs or societies, leisure or cultural activities, or entertainments.

Complaints on this subject were collected by O. Banks, who showed, for example, how difficult it is for shift workers to know in advance what their rest days will be, because of the uncertainties associated with shift rotation schemes: as is well known, shift schedules may be changed during the year or even in the course of a month, so that it is often difficult to make plans for more than a fortnight ahead. One special, but important disadvantage was mentioned by H. Brown, namely the impossibility of attending evening classes.

M. Maurice and C. Monteil presented, in their study, a whole range of results that provide a good illustration of this type of difficulty. Thus, the greater the constraints imposed by the work schedules, the greater the interference with leisure. Among workers on a two-shift system, 29 per cent stated that there was "very great" or "fairly great" interference with leisure activities. The corresponding figure was 49 per cent for workers on a semi-continuous three-shift system and 62 per cent for the continuous three-shift system.

The same authors point out that the types of activity carried out by shift workers when they have some free time are most often those centred on the family and domestic life: many go in for "do it yourself" at home, gardening, animal breeding, or work on the land. These are somewhat solitary free activities (these results

support those obtained by Caillot).   These are also the main
activities on rest days during the week.   It would also appear
that, among shift workers, as compared with other workers, there
are more escapist forms of behaviour ("getting some fresh air",
"getting out of the house", "thinking of nothing"), as if, more
than other workers, they needed to free themselves from the constraints of their working life.

Finally, mention should be made of the importance of second
jobs (various forms of "double-jobbing");   double-jobbing is both
financially rewarding and compensatory.   The boundaries between
certain types of odd job work and paid employment are often very
vague.   In contrast, the same inquiry failed to show any appreciable difference between workers on normal day work and shift
workers in the extent to which they belonged to organisations, the
proportion belonging to organisations being generally very low.

In the inquiry relating to the United States, on the contrary,
a significant difference was found between these two categories of
workers: a higher proportion of workers on normal day work belonged
to two or three voluntary associations (it is true that in the
United States there is generally a greater degree of participation
in voluntary associations than in Europe).   Neither age nor level
of education changed this relation appreciably.   In the same way,
day workers tended to have greater responsibilities in voluntary
associations, and to devote more time to them than shift workers.
Here again, these relationships were not affected by any other
factor (age, education).   The same inquiry confirmed the results
of the French inquiry in respect of the types of activity carried
out and preferred by shift workers.   These were most often
"solitary" activities such as shooting, fishing and gardening.
Shift workers also complained that they were unable to watch
television programmes regularly.

The Social Dimension of Time

It may well be thought surprising that careful inquiry has
failed to show any difference in social participation between shift
workers and those on normal day work.   Such a finding would seem
to contradict the usual view of shift work, which tends to emphasise
the serious disadvantages of this method of working from the point
of view of community life.   How can this divergence be explained?
First of all, there is often a failure to make any real comparison
of the behaviour of shift workers with that of workers on normal
day work.   Several inquiries in which such a comparison was made,
however, showed that participation in social life, particularly in
the form of organised activities, was slight in both cases, informal
activities being most commonly in the majority.   In contrast, when
these two categories of workers are compared, it is found that
activities connected with the family and with domestic life are of
considerable importance in the populations studied (generally consisting of wage earners).   In this case, however, significant
differences in behaviour do appear among them, and provide confirmation of the social harmfulness of shift work.   It has often been
pointed out that workers generally make the home, rather than the
community, their centre of interest.   The majority of the inquiries
conducted among the working class have shown that little importance

is attached to specifically leisure activities, particularly of
the organised variety.   Family life, and work, including odd jobs[1]
done at home or work on another job, are of more interest to them.

The survey carried out by Maurice and Monteil showed clearly
that the workers' feelings about the drawbacks of shift work varied
according to the aspect of their life that was interfered with:
they were most sensitive to interference with family life, and somewhat less so with regard to interference with leisure activities
and relations with friends, in that order.   The greater a worker's
opposition to shift work the more he felt the interference, particularly with regard to leisure and relations with friends.
These results are in line with those of Mott and Mann, in the
inquiry already mentioned.

It is necessary, in addition, however, to emphasise a point
that is not always revealed by the inquiries: it is important to
distinguish between how individuals actually behave and how they
feel that they are able to act in some particular sphere.   In the
case of shift workers, the fact that they are aware that they cannot
participate in some forms of activity (especially in the case of an
activity to which a high value is attached in the life of the
community) is just as important as the behaviour actually observed.

The degree of constraint·felt by shift workers, even if only
purely subjective in character, is nevertheless one of the drawbacks of this method of working, and it is already known that this
feeling of alienation may contribute towards the development of
certain psychosomatic disorders.

The general feeling most commonly expressed of "not living
like other people", of having "a different way of life", or of
being "shut off from normal life" is linked to a large extent with
this psychological factor.   Even if these are thought to be
"stereotypes", it must be remembered that such stereotypes may
play an important part in determining the extent to which shift
work is accepted and in the adjustment of the worker and his
family to that kind of work.   All attempts to improve shift work
systems in order to reduce their harmfulness must aim at reducing
to a minimum the gap between shift workers and those considered as
leading a "normal" life.

The significance of the concept of "normal life" itself then
calls for examination, particularly in relation to the concept of
time.   A certain paradox can be observed in industrial society:
technical progress and the development of the economic organisation of society tend to reduce the importance of work as compared
with the time spent away from work (too often equated with
leisure), but, at the same time, the opportunities actually
available for taking advantage of free time for the development
of the personality by participation in social life are continually
becoming fewer.

---

[1] See A. Touraine: La société postindustrielle (Paris,
Denoël, 1969), "Loisirs, participation, innovation", pp. 261-306.

What do we mean, therefore, when we speak of the use of time?
Is this time lost or gained, and by whom?   Durkheim, in his
classic Les formes élémentaires de la vie religieuse, published in
1912, distinguished between "sacred" and "profane" time.   In this
connection he wrote that the division of time into days, weeks,
months, years, etc., corresponded to a periodicity of rites, feast
days and public ceremonies.   A calendar was the expression of the
pattern of group activities, while at the same time its function
was to ensure that they took place at regular intervals.   Sorokin[1],
in turn, describing the origin of the concept of time, distinguished
between "mechanical" time (as measured by clocks) and "socio-
cultural time", the former being continuous, the latter discontinuous
(certain group activities may follow one another without a break, but
others follow one another after more or less regular intervals).
The unity of time, in the latter case, is generally marked by
feasts, rites or customs that may vary in duration.   For this
author, as for Durkheim, time provides the means of ensuring the
regularity of group activities.   The concept of socio-cultural
time may therefore vary in character, depending on whether a small
group is involved (members of a family, or inhabitants of a district), a complex organisation, or a society, but in each case this
concept is related to group activities (see also Blakelock).

Thus the predictability of the behaviour of individuals is
linked to the state of social organisation: the greater the degree
of organisation, the greater is the ability to forecast.   Talcott
Parsons[2] shares this point of view when he says that lack of
predictability of the behaviour of others is one of the characteristics of the state of "anomie", i.e. of an absence of social
organisation.   These concepts, namely those of mechanical and
socio-cultural time, and that of the regularity of activities
that results in both cases, may be useful for the purposes of this
study.   Thus the shift system may be considered as a mechanical
time system that clashes with a system of socio-cultural time.
The difficulties encountered and caused by shift work would then
correspond to a displacement, a break or even a conflict between
these two types of time.   The mechanical time of work organisation
could also be considered as a "bureaucratic" time that is the
expression of the "culture" of the industrial organisation;   it is
also that of the economist, to whom the concept of social time is
foreign, since he is unable to assign a value to it.

Another approach to time introduces a complementary point of
view.   Time may be interpreted and considered as a system of
exchange.   It will therefore provide a means of acquiring goods
of varying value ("time is money").   Thus time may be exchanged
for activities or non-activities.   The same amount of time, when
"spent", may provide goods in varying amounts, depending on the
socio-professional status of the individual concerned.   The
quality of the time may also come into play.   For the worker on
night work, for example, the quality of his time during the day is
greatly reduced.   When he leaves work at 4 o'clock in the morning,

---

[1] Sorokin: Sociocultural causality, space, time (London,
Cambridge University Press, 1943).

[2] Parsons: The social system (Glencoe (Illinois), The Free
Press, 1951).

his first few hours of free time do not have a high exchange value
in relation to social activities, and the same applies when he has
rest days during the week. Numerous examples of this type could
be given. Of importance here is only that an analysis of the concept of time from the point of view of quantity and quality would
make it possible to assess the working and non-working time of the
shift worker, and to appreciate, with greater understanding, the
difficulties that he meets with regard to socio-cultural time,
which he correctly considers to be that of normal life, since that
time corresponds, in fact, to the cultural characteristics of the
society to which he belongs or to which he aspires.

Another aspect of the use of time that calls for consideration
is that of flexibility. Certain activities are more or less
"flexible" than others, in the sense that they are not linked to
fixed rhythms or to a rigidly determined segment of time. Visiting
friends, or reading, listening to music or taking a walk are more
flexible activities than, for example, eating meals with the family,
sleeping, or watching a television programme. Flexibility may
depend both on the degree of institutionalisation of the activities
and the number of people involved (for example, attendance at a
football match or at the monthly meeting of an association). This
concept of flexibility has been used in the study of multiple shift
systems, among others by Blakelock and by Vroom.

The latter has constructed a model whereby the satisfaction of
the worker, in relation to the shift system, can be predicted. The
basic concept used by Vroom is what he has called the time pattern
for an activity, i.e., the time sequence corresponding to a particular activity. From this is derived the probability that an
activity will or will not be carried out at different times of day.
The concept of the flexibility of activities is thus arrived at by
a different route. Let us consider, for example, three types of
activity: A = very flexible activity (one that may be carried out
at any hour of the day or night), B = moderately flexible activity
(one that can be carried out only during part of the day), and
C = very inflexible activity (one that is restricted to a precise
time of day). The following diagram is then obtained:

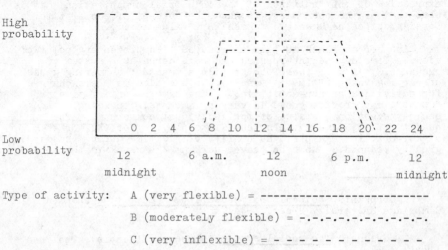

Certain activities, such as hobbies, are very flexible; others are moderately so, such as making certain kinds of purchases or dealings with the authorities; yet others, however, are limited in time, as for example, watching a particular television programme, attending the meetings of an association or going to the theatre.

If the work schedules of the different shifts that a worker on a continuous three-shift rota will have to work (for example, night shift 10 p.m. to 6 a.m., morning shift 6 a.m. to 2 p.m. and afternoon shift 2 to 10 p.m.) are included in the diagram just given, it will become clear that the probability of carrying out certain types of activity are largely determined by the shift on which he is working. Thus certain activities will be possible only every three weeks. It would then be possible to predict the over-all satisfaction of a shift worker in terms of the activities that he values the most, or which are valued most highly by his group or by the community to which he belongs. Two persons working on the same time schedule may or may not be satisfied, depending on the value that they assign to certain types of activity. Vroom gives the following example: a person who actively participates in the activities of a local association, which, it is assumed, take place in the evening, will be rather dissatisfied with working on the afternoon shift, while somebody who likes to go shooting or fishing in his free time will no doubt prefer that shift.

Although the theories of this author are based on a psycho-logical analysis of satisfaction, the concepts that he uses are applicable in sociological analysis and are related to the concept of time found in Durkheim and Sorokin.

These considerations are of interest in the analysis of the various aspects of shift work in a wider context than usual. They enable us, above all, to go beyond industrial organisation as such and to take into account the whole sphere of life outside work, where the shift worker (often considered as an individual living on the margin of society) encounters the life of the community in all its complexity, and where the mechanical time of the organiser of work meets the socio-cultural time of man as a social being.

CHAPTER VI

WORKERS' ATTITUDES

In the preceding chapters, an attempt has been made to evaluate the main repercussions of shift work on the behaviour of workers in the factory, the family, and society, not only from the physiological and medical point of view but also from that of social relations. The general conclusion that would seem to emerge from the information presented so far is as follows: shift work as a way of organising the use of time, disturbs not only the social relations and the everyday behaviour of the workers and their families but also the fundamental physiological rhythms of the human body. It would seem desirable for the study of shift work to be carried out in the future on the basis of the concept of time, whether the mechanical time of the work organiser or the economist, or the socio-cultural time of the psychologist or sociologist. One question that crops up at this stage, arising from the conflict between these two interpretations of time, is that of the relationship between economic logic and social logic. Before that question is answered, however, it is important to know how the workers react to this method of working: do they accept or reject it? What are their preferences with regard to the different systems? Do they feel that it has any advantages for them, or mainly drawbacks? All these questions call for an answer, if solutions are to be found to the problems mentioned previously.

In order to interpret attitudes of acceptance or rejection of shift work, reference will have to be made to the information already presented, but also to other aspects of the situation, such as the financial advantages generally associated with this method of working for those who are obliged to accept it. Although they are paid at special rates, the result is always ambiguous, since such rates serve both as compensation and as an incentive.

The presentation of the results of recent surveys will make it easier to appreciate the effect of shift work on the worker's social life and to emphasise the extent to which life at work and life outside it continually interact with one another.

Many of the studies previously presented took into account the workers' opinions with regard to shift work, but some of them showed a lack of agreement between the opinions of the workers and the objective conditions as determined by scientific study.

Wyatt and Marriott[1] were surprised by the contradiction between what the workers felt and what they did. In the course of an inquiry conducted in three metallurgical factories, 34 per cent of the workers said that they disliked the night shift because they did not obtain sufficient sleep, 23 per cent because of the changes in social habits, and 23 per cent because of nutritional and digestive disoders. Over-all, 80 per cent of the workers felt that they were more tired when they were on the night shift, particularly around 3 o'clock in the morning. When a long cycle of rotation was used (a month or a fortnight), fatigue tended to increase as the weeks passed. The sensation of fatigue was also felt towards the end of the weeks on

---

[1] For the complete list of references to this chapter, see part III of appendix 5.

day work, no doubt because of the workers' apprehension about starting night work again. When asked for information on sleep disturbances associated with changes of shift, about half of the workers stated that they were able to adjust fairly quickly.

These results show the importance of subjective factors in fatigue, as emphasised by psychologists and psychiatrists. Workers who have been on this method of working for a long time consider that they have adjusted to it. Even among those who are hostile to night work, few try to have themselves transferred to other work. Account must be taken, however, in these reactions, of the financial advantages of shift work, and particularly of night work, and also of a certain resistance to change. When habits have been acquired, there is a fear of having to develop new ones.

The inquiry of Burger and his co-workers, conducted in 1955 among two groups of workers on different systems of rotation, stressed the psychological characteristics that determine the attitude of workers to shift work. The major physiological disorders were most commonly found among the asthenic and appeared rather to be the projection of some form of psychological maladjustment to the whole range of conditions of work. These authors also noted that a positive attitude on the part of the members of the family could help the worker to adjust better.

In contrast, the study carried out by W. A. Hogg in 1961 in the United States among 1,686 workers in an oil refinery demonstrated the existence of a whole range of external factors favourable to the workers' adjustment. Those who worked on shifts had better working conditions than the others (monitoring work not requiring physical effort, well-equipped premises sheltered against bad weather). Working in small groups, they had a greater feeling of responsibility for their work, and a sense of holding key positions in the plant. Finally, the refinery having recently been constructed in a brand new town ("a three-shift city"), the facilities were designed to make life easier for the shift workers and their families.

It may be considered, therefore, that the importance of the three-shift work schedule in this town had determined, to a certain extent, the pattern of life in the community, thus reducing the usual feeling of living on the margin of society. These favourable conditions, of course, do not completely eliminate the harmful effects and the social cost of this method of working, but they do significantly reduce the difficulties workers have in adjusting to shift work.

The results of the studies mentioned could be repeated many times over. In fact, research on the physiological and medical effects of shift work often includes opinion surveys based on interviews or conversations with the workers. In general, however, such surveys are of limited value because of the small size of the samples or the impossibility of allowing for major variables such as age, seniority in shift work, working conditions and so on.

The results of certain surveys of the attitudes of the workers to shift work and its methods of operation will now be considered. Wherever possible, reference will be made to the more fragmentary results of other studies. An account will be given, in succession, of the attitudes of the workers to the methods of organisation and operation of shift work systems, and then of their general attitudes of acceptance or rejection of this method of working, and the reasons put forward.

Reactions to Particular Features
of Shift Work

One of the aims of the survey conducted by M. Maurice and
C. Monteil was to analyse the attitudes of the workers with regard
to the way in which shift work is organised, by the comparison of
groups of workers employed under different systems. The sample of
workers, of whom there were 800, interviewed in five undertakings,
included 24 per cent of workers on normal day work, 19 per cent
employed on two 8-hour shifts, 13 per cent on a semi-continuous
three-shift system, 26 per cent on continuous three-shift system
and 18 per cent on permanent day or night shifts.

The over-all results of this survey confirm certain results
obtained in other studies, but their greatest interest lies in the
reasons the workers gave for their views in particular situations.
Considered in isolation, attitudes may sometimes appear contradictory,
without a detailed knowledge of the position of the individual concerned. However, the results reproduced below can provide a lead
for the establishment of general principles, provided that certain
aspects of the situation (work schedule, location of the undertaking,
age and seniority) are taken into account in the interpretation of
the workers' responses.

The night shift always appears to be the decisive factor in the
workers' attitudes towards shift work. The ability to adjust may
vary from individual to individual, some preferring frequent changes
and others not. It would seem, therefore, that the selection of
workers for this method of working and the choice of the shift rotation system should take into account individual characteristics,
the working conditions peculiar to each undertaking, and the particular way of life of the local community.

Preferred Shifts

On the whole, the morning shift was the one preferred.[1] Other
surveys including that of H.G. Brown, have mentioned the same
preference. The morning shift frees the afternoon for other occupations, and interferes only to a limited extent with sleep; moreover,
in this case it is possible to go to bed earlier. Among the reasons
put forward for the preference for the morning shift, 38 per cent
concerned free time, 20 per cent family life, 15 per cent fatigue
and 9 per cent social life. To have the afternoon and the evening
free seemed to be greatly appreciated.

In contrast, when the afternoon shift is preferred, the reasons
given mainly concerned fatigue or health (76 per cent). In this
case, the individuals concerned no doubt dislike getting up early,
especially if they live far from their place of work. This was the case
for example, in this survey, of women who, working in the textile
industry, often live in a neighbouring mining area where there is
no work for them.

---

[1] Morning shift, 52 per cent; afternoon shift, 33 per cent;
night shift, 5 per cent; no preferences, 10 per cent.

Preference for the night shift is found in a minority of individuals, and the reasons given are more varied. In addition to the financial advantages (bonus for night work), both objective and subjective reasons are put forward: better working conditions, absence of supervisory personnel, more team spirit, and the feeling that "time passes more quickly".

Workers on permanent night shift of course mention the free time during the day, as well as a decrease in fatigue. It is true that, in certain cases where supervisory work is involved, the workload is smaller than during the day. The absence, or reduction in the numbers, of supervisory staff also gives the feeling of greater freedom at work.

Changeovers

The question has been raised whether changes of shift are felt by the individuals concerned as uniformly unpleasant, or whether the difficulties vary. In general, whatever the rotation pattern used, changes involving the night shift are felt as being the most tiring; this is particularly true of changes from the morning or afternoon shift to the night shift. The reality of the fatigue engendered by shift changes has been confirmed by the physiological studies considered previously.

Ease of adjustment depends on the shift system concerned. Thus, in the case of the three-shift system, it is considered that adjustment is very easy for a two-day period, whereas this is not the case with a two-shift system. The table given below shows clearly the differences that exist in this connection between the different systems.

Proportion of workers stating that they have had
difficulty in adjusting to rotating shift work,
by type of schedule and time needed to adjust
(percentages)

Type of schedule	Time needed to adjust		
	2 days or less	3 days	4 days or more
Two shift	49	38	12
Semi-continuous three-shift	37	37	26
Continuous three-shift	27	34	27

It is clear that many factors may affect the worker's adjustment. Thus it has been found that, for a given schedule, workers in the chemical industry adjust more rapidly to changes of shift than those in the iron and steel or car industries. This may be related to the workload, which is heavier in the case of the last two industries, while in the chemical industry the workload is lower in many jobs (monitoring, for example), and involves a different type of fatigue. Age is another factor: difficulties of adjustment are

most commonly reported by the youngest workers, whereas a certain
degree of habituation to changes of shift may develop with age
or length of service.

Scheduled Hours

When workers are asked about the arrangement of the daily
hours of work, and particularly about starting and stopping times,
it is found that the majority prefer the existing schedule. There
can be no doubt that workers often simply fear change, whatever
it may be. To the extent that they have no power of decision, or
even an opportunity to express their opinions, change remains an
unknown quantity for them. They therefore prefer to stick to what
they know and to a situation to which they are accustomed, even if
they consider it to be unsatisfactory. However, those who spend
more time travelling between home and place of work prefer later
starting times for the morning shift. Factories located in rural
areas often have work schedules that start earlier than those
located in urban areas. In the latter case, the times at which
public transport services operate have to be taken into account,
whereas in rural areas the workers are generally picked up by a
bus service operated by the undertaking. In addition, rural workers
may be accustomed to an early morning start.

Frequency of Rotation

Another important factor in the organisation of shift work is
the frequency of rotation. A weekly frequency is generally used,
but shorter frequencies do exist (two or three days), as well as
longer ones (a fortnight or a month). When asked about this, the
majority of workers state that they do not wish to change the
frequency of rotation with which they are familiar. However, a
minority would prefer frequencies of rotation longer than those
that are being used, in this case longer than a week.

What are the reasons for these attitudes? When a frequency
longer than a week is preferred, it is considered that this would
facilitate physiological adjustment to changes of shift, or that
the night shift would have to be worked less frequently during the
cycle of rotation. In contrast, when a frequency of less than a
week (two or three days) is preferred, this is because the worker
prefers to work for a shorter period of time on the night shift,
either for health reasons or for ease of adaptation, or because
this system enables him to intersperse rest days more frequently
among the working days.

Desired Changes

Attention will now be devoted to the suggestions made by the
workers themselves for improving the operation of the shift system.

One initial result must be emphasised: as compared with those
of workers on a two-shift system, the suggestions made by workers
on continuous three-shift working call for a much more radical
reorganisation of shift work. This is no doubt the reflection of
an increase in the constraints imposed, and therefore of an
increasing involvement of the individuals concerned in the schedule
operated.

Certain suggestions concern changes within existing systems,
such as changes in starting times. Depending on the local situation,
a preference may be expressed for starting the morning shift earlier
or later; others point out the advantage that would be gained by
reducing the duration of the night shift. In contrast, suggestions
that the frequency of rotation should be changed, or the night shift
eliminated, imply a more fundamental reorganisation. It is also often
suggested that the hours of work should be reduced and an additional
crew brought in. The latter type of suggestion is most frequently
made by workers on continuous three-shift working.

Acceptance of Shift Work as Such

Once the opinions of the workers with regard to the methods
of organisation of shift work have been considered, the next question
concerns their degree of satisfaction with respect to this method of
working. Are they in favour of shift work as such? What are the
reasons for their attitudes? Under what conditions are they more
or less favourable towards this method of organisation? All these
questions are of central importance to any study of shift work.
Not only do they enable us to appreciate the human and social cost
of this method of working, but they may also contribute to improving
its organisation, and they form part of the more general study of
the working and living conditions of the workers. Shift work, in
fact, provides research in social science with an almost experimental
situation for the study of the interactions between life at work and
life outside it, whereas the various aspects of the workers' life are
all too often artificially isolated and sufficient account is not
taken of the unity of living and working conditions.[1]

Most of the studies of shift work have shown that the majority
of the workers are more or less dissatisfied with it.[2] What,
however, does this dissatisfaction mean? It is no doubt quite normal
for a method of working that tends to isolate the worker from the way
of life of his surroundings not to have his full support. Nevertheless, the opportunities for choice on the part of the worker must not
be over-estimated: shift work is most commonly only one aspect of
working conditions, among others, one factor in a situation that the
worker has to accept or reject as a whole.

---

[1] This point has been frequently stressed by Georges Friedmann.
See in particular Le travail en miettes (Paris, Gallimard, 1966).

[2] See Organisation for European Economic Co-operation:
Travailleurs de l'acier et progrès technique, Rapport comparatif
sur six enquêtes nationales (Paris, 1959); Floyd C. Mann and
L. Richard Hoffman: Automation and the worker (New York,
Henry Holt, 1960); G. H. Bast: Ploegenarbeid in de industrie
(Arnhem, Contractgroepvereniging Productiviteit, Van Loghum Staterus,
1960); P. E. Mott, Floyd C. Mann, Q. McLoughlin and D. Warwick:
Shift work: The social, psychological and physical consequences
(Ann Arbor, University of Michigan Press, 1965); Naville and
co-workers: L'automation et le travail humain, op cit., and Grossin:
Le travail et le temps, op cit.

In contrast, the study of the motives of the minority group of those who are satisfied with shift work, or who have been able to choose this method of working, would also enable us to understand better the reasons for the dissatisfaction of the majority.

In this connection, the inquiries of Floyd C. Mann and L.R. Hoffmann and of M. Maurice and C. Monteil have provided useful information. Thus the French inquiry (1965) was concerned with the reasons given by the workers for wishing to continue or to give up shift work. This was no doubt a hypothetical situation, but one that made it possible to analyse in considerable detail the attitudes of the workers as a function of a number of situational variables. Answers to the question "Would you like to continue shift work in the future, or not?" are shown in the table given below, as a percentage of the replies, for the different shift systems.

Work schedule	Yes, without hesitation	Yes, with hesitation	No	No reply
Permanent shift	68	12	19	1
Rotating two-shift	65	16	17	2
Semi-continuous rotating three-shift	33	25	41	1
Continuous rotating three-shift	32	35	33	-

The high proportion of replies classified as "yes, with hesitation" may appear surprising. As will be seen later, this reply reflects the ambiguous situation of the worker who accepts this method of working on account of a whole range of constraints, particularly of a financial nature. This type of reply is more frequent for schedules that give certain financial advantages (semi-continuous and continuous three-shift systems).

What are the reasons given, for the different categories of reply and work schedule?

When a worker wishes to continue shift work in the future ("yes, without hesitation"), the main reasons given relate to "free time" and "habit", in the majority of cases. The free time provided by shift work is appreciable, in fact, whatever the schedule; there is even more free time on permanent shifts or on the two-shift system. "Habit" reflects rather a certain degree of habituation or resistance to change. When a worker has organised his existence around a certain type of schedule, he will hesitate when faced by the effort involved in reorganisation, especially since the other members of the family will also be affected. A special reason comes into play in the case of the semi-continuous or continuous three-shift system - wages, or in other words the financial benefits granted in the form of bonuses.

The positive replies, but "with hesitation", reveal the dilemma that confronts shift workers who find it hard to strike a balance between the advantages of shift work (free time or earnings) and disadvantages (fatigue due to age, state of health, constraints imposed by night work, and disturbances of family life). The

positive character of the reply is thus considerably attenuated by
this whole range of reservations. Fatigue is mentioned particularly
by those working under a three-shift system, while age only
accentuates this tendency.

As far as those who do not wish to continue shift work are
concerned, their reasons are more or less the same as those previously mentioned, except that the disadvantages from the point of
view of family life are mentioned more often and the emphasis placed
on health, fatigue and age is even greater.

Certain variables (age, skill, marital status) may affect the
above-mentioned tendencies. Thus, the higher the level of skill,
the greater the desire to give up shift work. Among workers on a
three-shift system, married workers most often wish to continue
with this method of working. Hesitation is most marked among the
youngest and the oldest workers.

On the assumption that, among the reasons that lead workers to
wish to do shift work, economic motives are comparatively important,
an additional question was asked in order to determine whether
this was in fact the case: "On the assumption that your wages
and your work remain the same, would you prefer to do shift work or
normal day work?"

The replies to this question are shown below as percentages:

Work schedule	Prefer normal day work	Prefer shift work	No reply
Permanent shift	19	72	9
Rotating two-shift	21	78	1
Semi-continuous rotating three-shift	67	30	3
Continuous rotating three-shift	63	34	3

These results would seem to confirm the hypothesis: those who
replied yes, with hesitation, did so mainly because of the financial
advantages of shift work. This was particularly true of workers on
a three-shift system. The fact nevertheless remains that one-third
wished, even for the same wages, to continue shift work. An
analysis of their motives should be particularly enlightening.

What were, then, the reasons given in this case? The trends
previously mentioned were even more strongly marked.

Thus, workers who opted for the same wages, for normal day
work, mentioned mainly the regular way of life, and particularly
the advantages from the point of view of family and social life,
as well as the preservation of health, while an overwhelming
majority of those who, even for the same wages, would have preferred
to continue shift work stressed the advantage of free time.

These results show that shift workers are generally subjected
to contradictory pressures: on the one hand there are financial
advantages (it will be seen later that the interest expressed in
free time is sometimes a cover for an interest in opportunities for
double-jobbing); and on the other hand there is the aspiration
towards a more normal and regular existence that permits a better
family and social life.

The effect of these opposing pressures is clearly reflected
among the minority of workers who admit to doing another job, in
addition to their main occupation. To the extent, in fact, that
shift work, whatever its form, makes free time available during
the day or during the week, this free time may provide the opportunity to take a second job.

Thus, in the course of the same inquiry, 21 per cent of those
interviewed admitted that they had another job. The proportion
obviously varied with the type of work schedule, as follows:

Work schedule	Percentages
Permanent shift.........................	12
Rotating two-shift......................	14
Semi-continuous rotating three-shift ...	27
Continuous rotating three-shift.........	33

It can be seen, therefore, that the importance of double-
jobbing increases with the type of rota that provides the most free
time during the day, or during the week (continuous three-shift).
It would thus seem that double-jobbing is one of the indicators of
the economic pressures that induce workers to accept shift work, or
to wish to continue with this method of working. A strong
correlation was found, in fact, between those who do a second job
and those who state that they have difficulty in making ends meet,
especially among workers on the continuous three-shift system:

Assessment of family budget	Workers having a second job (as a percentage)
"No problems"	19
"Tight"	39
"Very tight"	50

Whereas 33 per cent of workers on a continuous three-shift rota
stated that they had a second job, this proportion increased to
50 per cent among those who said that they had difficulty in making
ends meet.[1]

_____

[1] It may also be assumed that the correlation between the three-
shift system and double-jobbing reflects the economic pressures to
which workers who show this dual behaviour are subjected.

Other results of the inquiry showed that it was precisely among this category of workers that the highest proportion was found of those who wished to continue with shift work, even at the same wage.

Shift work would thus seem to be particularly attractive to persons subjected to economic pressures, not only because of the financial advantages that it brings (bonuses and allowances) but also because by leaving more time free, it enables them to take a second job. Even if, in this latter case, only a minority of individuals is involved, this may influence the motives of those who wish to continue with shift work.

Such an analysis, of course, reveals the relativity of individual choices. Other studies would be necessary in order to explore the causes of the economic pressures to which certain categories of workers are subjected. Nevertheless, the results of this inquiry tend to show that those involved are generally married persons in that phase of the life cycle associated with the greatest economic constraints (young children, wage still relatively low, middle age).

The inquiry carried out by Floyd C. Mann and L.R. Hoffmann[1] in two power stations (1960) also showed the negative attitudes of workers with regard to shift work. Thus the majority replied in the negative to the question: "If you were a young man, would you take a job requiring you to work shifts?"

This study was less concerned with the methods of organisation of shift schedules than that mentioned previously; nevertheless, it did show that shift work seemed to be better tolerated in the plant with a weekly frequency of rotation than in the one with a monthly frequency. When a choice was offered between shift rotation and permanent shifts, the workers on the monthly rota were more in favour of permanent shifts than the others. The authors pointed out, however, that the choice of permanent shifts may perhaps be a way of escaping from the problems associated with shift rotation, without necessarily being a realistic attitude. Other results from the same inquiry showed that satisfaction with shift work tended to increase with length of shift work service. Nevertheless, it is possible that, with time, a selection process takes place that tends to eliminate the workers who have adjusted least well to this method of working, and thereby increases the proportion of those who are able to adjust. The authors stressed the importance of long-term studies aimed at eliminating this selection effect, which could provide useful information on the development of attitudes and the conditions for adaptation.

In a more recent study, Mott, Mann, McLoughlin and Warwick[2] investigated in more detail the psychological effects of shift work, namely the extent to which this method of working may affect the mental health of the workers. Certain results of their inquiry call for mention here, since they provide information on work adjustment and satisfaction as regards shift work. Thus, the effect of shift

[1] Mann and Hoffman, op. cit.

[2] Mott et al., op cit.

work on mental health was most marked in the case of the youngest, better educated workers, with young children, and without a long period of shift work service. In contrast, those with a second job were less disturbed by the difficulties encountered. The authors considered that, in this case, the workers accepted the constraints imposed by shift work more easily, since this system enabled them to achieve personal objectives. The authors also emphasised, correctly, the factors that may facilitate the workers' adjustment particularly a favourable attitude on the part of the other members of the family.

A Closer Look at Psychological Adjustment

It is clearly difficult to formulate any generally applicable conclusions on the basis of the results presented here. That, however, was not the intention. In the present state of research in the social sciences, one can hope to arrive at general propositions only when an accumulation of data from numerous studies is available, and above all, only after the relevant problems have been formulated in relation to the subject of the research; it must be admitted, however, that the study of shift work is still far from satisfying these requirements. The purpose of presenting the results of the studies carried out so far was merely to enable certain questions to be asked, certain problems to be stated, and certain fields of research to be defined.

This may seem disappointing to the man of action, the man responsible for getting things done, but a more rapid approach would only create the illusion that solutions capable of application had already been found; and this would not be satisfactory either for the social sciences or for those concerned with industrial practice. Nevertheless, agreement already seems to have been reached on certain points, on the basis of certain observations that are similar in character and are reflected in the workers' own opinions.

Especially in the case of the three-shift system[1], shift work certainly constitutes one of the most abnormal and unsettling kinds of industrial employment from the point of view of the workers' physical and mental well-being and from that of their participation in the life of the community. Now that attention has been given to the effects of this method of working on the health of the workers, there should be greater awareness of the often serious disadvantages of shift work for family and social life. It is probably in this respect that shift work results in the greatest number of potential conflicts, as a result of the disparity between the way of life of the workers concerned and that of their friends and relations.[2]

One must not generalise, of course. The majority of authors stress the whole range of factors affecting the physiological, psychological and social adaptation of the workers. As pointed out

---

[1] A clear distinction must be made between the two-shift system and the three-shift system; the latter, because it involves a night shift, is that most commonly accused of having harmful effects.

[2] Andlauer and Fourre, op. cit., p. 148.

by Andlauer and Fourre[1], many problems are inter-related with
those of the three-shift system, on which their effects are
superimposed, so that its specific consequences would seem
difficult to define. They would doubtless appear less important
if it was possible to allow for related factors, such as the
journey to work, housing conditions, the organisation of rest periods,
second jobs, and leisure activities, which could be the subject
of measures unconnected with the employment relationship.

In order to measure the human and social cost of shift work,
attention must therefore be paid to the whole range of living
and working conditions that may help or hinder the workers'
adjustment. Even if the worker states that he is satisfied with
this system and finds that it has certain advantages, this is not
enough to demonstrate that a real adjustment has occurred, particularly from the physiological point of view.

The problem of double-jobbing (sometimes also called
"moonlighting") is a good example of this. It is well known that
the opportunity for taking a second job may lead to a preference
for shift work, but the question then arises of the effects, both
in the short and in the long term, of an excessive workload on the
health of the individual concerned, and therefore of the costs that
will ultimately have to be borne by society. While the immediate
interests of the individual may seem to be in harmony with those of
industry, it is possible that in the medium term such a situation
may have certain repercussions on the national economy. This is
an example of the limitations of the traditional economic calculations that fail to take account of the human and social cost of
work (for example, "cost of illness" or "hospital costs" are considered separately from "productivity of undertakings" or "economic
growth").

This means that in assessing the costs and benefits of shift
work, the results of opinion surveys must be interpreted with caution
and viewed within their economic and social context.

Thus a better adjustment and a more positive attitude on the
part of the workers has sometimes been found in industries or
communities in which shift work has always existed; this method
of working is not then the concern of a minority, but forms part of
the accepted occupational and social norms. Such situations, of
course, do not eliminate the harmful effects of shift work, but
may reduce them. The way in which social life is organised in the
community may thus facilitate the social participation of workers
on a three-shift rota. This may be the case in industries
traditionally located in rural areas (iron and steel works, paper
works, textile factories, etc.). In contrast, the attitude of the
workers will often be less positive in the case of undertakings
where shift work has recently been adopted, or factories located
in urban areas; in the latter case the shift worker will certainly
feel more strongly that he is living on the margin of society as
a whole.

---

[1] Andlauer and Fourre, op. cit., p. 149.

It would be preferable, in many cases, to speak of habituation rather than adjustment. For many workers, pressure in opposing directions may make themselves felt. After weighing up the positive and negative aspects of shift work, the worker resignedly accepts his current situation: confronted by a change that remains an unknown quantity for him, he prefers a situation to which he is more or less accustomed, often at the cost of a major effort in the organisation of his life and that of his family. It should not be thought on that account, however, that such a situation is satisfactory either for the individual or for society.

It should not be concluded either that the complaints of the workers are only "stereotypes", as did Dr. Bast[1] at the end of his important study, and that solutions can be found by eliminating the resulting rationalisations. The difficulties encountered by the workers, their feelings and their attitudes with regard to shift work, deserve as much consideration as the technical and economic factors that affect the decision to adopt this form of work organisation.

Opinion surveys, however, to which research is often restricted, are not adequate in themselves to enable the whole range of these social factors to be understood and interpreted. Other approaches must be adopted in combination, so that a socio-economic analysis of shift work can be undertaken. The importance of the questions raised in this field is such that partial answers, or purely local solutions, will serve only to hide the real problems. Here as elsewhere, ready-made solutions are all too often adopted to enable the workers to adjust to the industrial situation in the light of economic requirements, whereas it would be preferable, in the light of social requirements, to try and modify the industrial situation as well, so as to decrease the social cost that such adjustment involves.

---

[1] Bast, op. cit.

CHAPTER VII

INSTITUTIONAL FACTORS

A brief description is given below of the main problems faced
by the employer in the introduction of shift work, and more generally
in its management and administration. The various aspects of
shift work have been considered in the preceding chapters, but
without any reference to the institutional factors peculiar to
each individual country. It is clear, however, that the organisation and operation of a shift work system cannot be envisaged
without reference to the labour standards in force in each country
and to the positions of the various labour organisations that may
oppose or promote the system. Moreover, in practice shift work
raises a large number of problems of management practice, such as
the calculation of the bonuses to be paid, the organisation of
the shifts in relation to fluctuations in the work, or the welfare
facilities required to meet the special needs of the workers concerned. In relation to all these problems, shift work may be
the subject of bargaining between employers and trade unions.

With an eye to the future, consideration should be given to
possible improvements in shift working and the best ways of bring-
ing them about. It is not possible in this field, any more than
in the others, to provide ready-made solutions or solutions that
are generally applicable: this is so because the situations vary
so much and the information on the various experiments carried out
in different undertakings is still insufficient in most cases to
allow useful conclusions to be drawn. However, it is possible to
appreciate the nature of the problems raised and to indicate
possible solutions on the basis of the information and suggestions
given below.

It may perhaps be of value to emphasise one particularly
important point. It seems that there has not been enough
systematic research on the organisation of shift work. Apart
from a few cases where the adoption of a shift rotation system was
based on medical considerations, or on consultation with the workers
after a trial period, decisions are most commonly taken on the
basis of existing practice or local customs. More experimentation
is desirable, if the whole range of problems raised by this method
of working is to be solved. It seems anomalous that this approach
should not be adopted in the case of the working and living conditions of the labour force, whereas it appears to be the norm when
attempts are made to improve technical processes or the productivity
or profitability of the undertaking.

Labour Standards

The labour standards affecting shift work may be contained in
legislation, collective agreements or international labour Conventions or other ILO instruments or recommendations. It would
appear that the main aim of labour standards has been to protect
certain categories of workers (children, young people and women)
whom it might be desired to employ on shifts, and that such protection has not been restricted to shift working in the case of hours
of work, rest and night work.

At first, financial compensation in various forms (bonuses and allowances) was provided to make up for the other drawbacks of shift work. Gradually, however, other measures came to be taken, such as a reduction in the hours of work which, for example in the form of additional days off or rest days, tends to improve work schedules by taking into account the health and social welfare of the workers instead of their financial interests alone. These recent trends, encouraged by the ILO recommendations concerned with the reduction of the hours of work, emerge in particular in collective agreements between employers and unions.

As regards labour legislation, its main purpose is the control of working conditions so as to ensure the moral, physical and social protection of the workers. Shift work confronts those responsible for legislation with a whole range of problems concerning, in particular, the number of hours of work per day and per week, night work, work on Sundays and public holidays, rest days and annual holidays, and the protection of women and young workers. In addition, these questions must be seen in the context of the broader social policy of each individual country or common to a group of countries (for example, the European Economic Community), aimed at improving conditions of work; the reduction of hours of work, for example, may form part of such a policy. Labour legislation itself is in a state of continuous development.

It would be impossible, of course, to examine here, for all countries, the aspects of labour legislation that have a bearing on shift work. The aim will rather be to show, by means of examples taken from different countries, how and in which particular ways it has gradually become possible to regulate the use of shift work through labour legislation.

In certain countries, such as France, the Federal Republic of Germany and the United States, this method of working is the subject of special provisions; in others, such as Belgium and the Netherlands, the legislation does not contain such special provisions, but lists, among the exemptions from the general provisions, a certain number of industries or undertakings in which, because of their nature, operations can neither be stopped nor delayed. It is therefore necessary to refer, in each country, to the general legislation on the length of the working day, night work and weekly rest in order to find, among the exemptions, those more particularly concerned with shift work.

In the majority of countries, special rules also exist as part of plant agreements or contracts, or of collective agreements applicable to a particular region or branch of industry.

Consideration will first be given to the aspects of the general legislation that could give rise to difficulties in relation to the requirements of shift work.

Hours of Work

In most countries normal hours of work are laid down by law. Provision is also made for the payment of overtime at a higher rate for hours worked in excess of the norm. In the past, while the general norm was 48 hours a week, the limit laid down for continuous operation was 56 hours a week (average for a period of three weeks with a three-shift system). When, after the economic depression of the 1930s, the general norm was reduced to 40 hours in certain countries, the norms applicable to shift work were most often reduced to an average of 42 hours a week. This change was made in various ways by the introduction of a fourth crew. It will be remembered that previously shift workers were at times obliged to work for as long as 16 hours at a stretch for purposes of shift rotation under a three-week cycle. The decrease in the hours of work therefore had a direct effect on the organisation of shift work.

The various stages of this development and its effects on shift work are reflected in the numerous texts adopted by the International Labour Conference, of which the earliest is the Hours of Work (Industry) Convention, 1919 (No. 1). Conventions applicable to particular industries, such as the Sheet-Glass Works Convention, 1934 (No. 43), and the Reduction of Hours of Work (Glass-Bottle Works) Convention, 1935 (No. 49), lay down special provisions. More recently, the Reduction of Hours of Work Recommendation, 1962 (No. 116) specified that special provisions might be formulated with regard to "processes which, by reason of their nature", had to be "carried on continuously by a succession of shifts". These special provisions should be so formulated that the average normal hours of work in continuous processes do not in any case exceed the normal hours of work fixed for the economic activity concerned.[1]

Works agreements or special provisions of collective agreements may, of course, regulate shift work more strictly than is provided for in international labour Conventions, or even in the legislation of the country concerned. The recent tendency for certain agreements to give shift workers preferential treatment from the point of view of hours of work may also be mentioned: in certain cases the average length of the working week for shift workers tends to be slightly less than that for the others. As will be seen later, trade union action has also been aimed at achieving a reduction in the hours of work of shift workers; this is the case, for example, in the iron and steel industry in the Federal Republic of Germany and, more recently, in France.

Weekly Rest

Together with night work, the weekly rest is undoubtedly one of the aspects of labour legislation that gives rise to the greatest difficulties in the introduction of shift work; the reference here, of course, is to the continuous or semi-continuous three-shift system.

In accordance with the standards and recommendations of the ILO, the majority of countries provide for an obligatory period of rest of at least 24 consecutive hours during each seven-day period; this period of rest must, in principle, coincide with the days established by the traditions or customs of the country or district. Provision has always been made for exemptions from this requirement, but only in a limited number of cases, where this is in the public interest or justified by technical requirements. Over the last

---

[1] See paragraph 13 (1) and (2) of the Recommendation.

few years, however, conditions have changed, particularly in the majority of the industrialised countries, and the taking of the weekly period of rest on various days of the week is tending to undermine the principle of Sunday as the day of rest. The legislation in force provides only a small degree of protection because the distinction between operations that have to be carried out on Sundays and those that do not is tending to become blurred.

The principles on which the legislation is based vary from country to country. In the Federal Republic of Germany and in the Netherlands, the legislation stresses the relation between the weekly period of rest and Sunday observance. When, as an exception, Sunday work is authorised, the aim of the legislation is not so much to ensure that, in compensation, a period of rest is taken on another day of the week, as to ensure that the maximum possible number of Sundays are free and that the number of hours worked on Sunday is limited. In France and Italy, by contrast, the legislation stresses the "weekly" character of the period of rest. It lays down that workers are entitled to a period of rest of 24 consecutive hours per week, taken "in principle" on Sundays. The exemptions are then mainly concerned with ensuring that a compensatory period of rest is taken during the week. The legislation of Belgium and Luxembourg falls between these two extremes.

The true importance of Sunday work cannot be measured merely by comparing the legislation in force in the various countries. Reference can sometimes be made to national statistics showing the proportion of undertakings or workers, in the various branches of industry or of economic activity, on continuous work and therefore operating on Sundays, but the statistics fail to cover certain types of work. As far as the lists of exemptions with regard to Sunday work are concerned, they do not always give an exact picture of the situation, since some of the items may now be out of date; special exemptions can always be granted on the grounds, in particular, of market conditions.

Of the countries of Western Europe, according to incomplete information supplied by the European Economic Community, France, the Federal Republic of Germany and the Netherlands are those having the highest rates of Sunday work, about 4 per cent of the working population being concerned. Preference for Sunday as the day of rest seems to have caused most difficulty, from the point of view of the extension of continuous operation, in the Federal Republic of Germany.

The principles applicable to the weekly period of rest are generally applicable to public holidays, of which the number and the distribution over the year vary from country to country; in this case also, the legislation provides for exemptions and for the corresponding compensation.

Night Work

The adoption of the three-shift system, whether semi-continuous or continuous, raises the problem of night work, and thereby again comes into conflict with general labour legislation.

Restrictions on night work relate essentially to women and young people; legislation for their protection has been introduced in many countries. The main outlines of the legislation were defined, from 1919 onwards, by the Night Work (Women) Convention, 1919 (No. 4) and the Night Work of Young Persons (Industry) Convention, 1919 (No. 6). These were revised in 1948 by Conventions Nos. 89 and 90, respectively, the most important provisions of which are given below:

Night Work (Women) Convention (Revised), 1948 (No. 89):

. . . .

Article 2

For the purpose of this Convention the term "night" signifies a period of at least eleven consecutive hours, including an interval prescribed by the competent authority of at least seven consecutive hours falling between ten o'clock in the evening and seven o'clock in the morning; the competent authority may prescribe different intervals for different areas, industries, undertakings or branches of industries or undertakings, but shall consult the employers' and workers' organisations concerned before prescribing an interval beginning after eleven o'clock in the evening.

Article 3

Women without distinction of age shall not be employed during the night in any public or private industrial undertaking or in any branch thereof, other than an undertaking in which only members of the same family are employed.

Night Work of Young Persons (Industry) Convention (Revised) 1948 (No. 90):

. . . .

Article 2

1.   For the purpose of this Convention the term "night" signifies a period of at least twelve consecutive hours.

2.   In the case of young persons under sixteen years of age, this period shall include the interval between ten o'clock in the evening and six o'clock in the morning.

3.   In the case of young persons who have attained the age of sixteen years but are under the age of eighteen years, this period shall include an interval prescribed by the competent authority of at least seven consecutive hours falling between ten o'clock in the evening and seven o'clock in the morning; the competent authority may prescribe different intervals for different areas, industries, undertakings or branches of industries or undertakings, but shall consult the employers' and workers' organisations concerned before prescribing an interval beginning after eleven o'clock in the evening.

Article 3

1.   Young persons under eighteen years of age shall not be
employed or work during the night in any public or private
industrial undertaking or in any branch thereof except as herein-
after provided for.

2.   For purposes of apprenticeship or vocational training in
specified industries or occupations which are required to be carried
on continuously, the competent authority may, after consultation
with the employers' and workers' organisations concerned, authorise
the employment in night work of young persons who have attained the
age of sixteen years but are under the age of eighteen years.

3.   Young persons employed in night work in virtue of the
preceding paragraph shall be granted a rest period of at least
thirteen consecutive hours between two working periods.

. . . .

A similar Convention (No. 79 of 1946), had already specified
the conditions applicable to night work for young persons in non-
industrial occupations.

In most countries, the legislation, based on the international
labour Conventions, provides for exemptions for certain industries
or services.   This is the case for industries or services where
night work is habitually or temporarily required;   they include
seasonal industries (food preservation, industrial establishments
for the processing of milk, etc.), services such as nursing services
or health services (hospitals, clinics), or public services (postal
and telegraph services) where female staff is employed.

Breaks and Rest Periods

Many of the Industrial Committees of the ILO have considered
the question of breaks and rest periods.   Thus, as early as 1950,
the Chemical Industries Committee submitted to the Governing Body
of the ILO a memorandum on questions concerning the organisation
of working hours[1], in which it asked, for shift workers, for a
break to enable each worker to take a meal.   The conclusions
adopted in 1963 by an ILO tripartite technical meeting for the
food products and drink industries call for "the establishment of
suitable rest periods for the workers on highly repetitive operations in order to relieve tension and monotony"[2].   These recommendations are usually taken into consideration in the works or
collective agreements in the various countries.   Their application
varies from industry to industry, and from region to region;   the
length of the breaks may be 20 to 30 or 40 minutes, depending on
the individual case.

---

[1] See Official Bulletin (Geneva, ILO), Vol. XXXIII, No. 4,
20 Dec. 1950, pp. 133-136.

[2] Ibid., Vol. XLVII, No. 2, Apr. 1964, p. 118.

Remuneration

Shift work gives rise to special problems of remuneration; these may relate to the special bonuses for night work, or for work done on Sundays or public holidays, or to the allowances paid as compensation, such as food allowances to compensate for the additional expenses associated with this method of working, such as meals eaten away from home. The ILO has also been concerned with this whole range of questions; for example in 1952 the Chemical Industries Committee, at its Third Session, adopted a resolution concerning the general problems of hours of work, which states that ".... the overtime rates and the rates for shift work should normally be determined, in accordance with the practice common in each country - by collective agreement, by arbitration award, or by laws and regulations".[1]

In 1962, at its Sixth Session, the same Committee adopted Conclusions (No. 44) on Principles and Methods for Determining Extra Rates for Shift Work: "Shift work .... causes inconveniences and expense to the worker and disturbs the normal conditions of his physical, family and social life; action should therefore be taken and research conducted to minimise any inconveniences which may arise from shift work." Recognising that the extent of these inconveniences may vary according to the circumstances, the Committee considered that "there should be adequate financial compensation". It distinguished, for this purpose, between the varying degrees of constraint imposed by shift work, as between double-day working (the afternoon shift is recognised as causing more inconvenience than the morning shift), semi-continuous working (the night shift causes most inconvenience), and finally continuous working, which combines all the inconvenience of the other systems, together with those of Sunday and weekend work.[2] In the same way, the Textiles Committee, at its 1963 session, and a tripartite technical meeting for the clothing industry held in 1964, stressed the need for special bonuses.[3]

These recommendations, as a whole, have been widely included in the labour legislation of collective agreements of individual countries. Such applications cannot be examined in detail here, since in any given country the provisions vary from industry to industry, or from region to region, depending on the system established by law or by collective agreements.

It should be noted, however, that in the calculation of overtime the number of hours worked per week is not generally taken as the starting point, but rather the average number of hours over the complete cycle of rotation.

---

[1] See Official Bulletin (Geneva, ILO), Vol. XXXV, No. 3, 20 Dec. 1952, p. 199.

[2] Ibid., No. XLV, No. 4, Oct. 1962, p. 300.

[3] Ibid., Vol. XLVI, No. 3, July 1963, p. 420; ibid., Vol. XLVII, No. 4, Oct. 1964, pp. 347-348.

The bonuses paid for shift work are generally determined by collective agreement or by works contract or agreement. Special methods of calculation of bonus payments are prescribed for shift work and are different for day work (morning and afternoon shifts), night work, and work on Sundays and public holidays. Several of these financial benefits may, of course, be combined: for example, a worker may simultaneously receive a bonus for night work, an allowance for additional expenditure on food, and bonuses for work under a system of continuous operation and for work on Sundays or public holidays.

The payment of special bonuses and allowances may, in addition, be combined with other benefits such as payment for time not worked (for example, a break or 20 or 30 minutes may be counted as time worked, so that payment is made for 8 hours but only 7 1/2 hours are worked[1]), free meals or meals at reduced prices for night workers, paid travelling time at certain times, or other facilities and welfare arrangements (rest room for use during breaks, quick service of hot meals and drinks, priority in the provision of housing close to the undertaking, transport services, emergency medical services and so on).

As far as bonuses are concerned, methods of calculation may vary from country to country and, in a given country, from industry to industry, or even from undertaking to undertaking.[2]

In the majority of countries, the bonuses or allowances are expressed either as a percentage of the normal wage for day work (they are then often derived from the basic wage) or as fixed amounts; these two methods may also be used in combination. Another form of compensation must also be mentioned that combines additional time off and higher wages: shift workers may work for a shorter number of hours (per day, week or month) than workers on normal day work. In other cases, and less frequently, the different shifts may have different hours of work. The evening and night shifts may then receive the same wage as the day shift, but work fewer hours; for example, eight hours' pay may be given for seven-and-a-half hours' work. This latter system is found, in particular, in Canada and the United States.

---

[1] It should be remembered that the length of the breaks and the remuneration vary from country to country, depending on the industries and categories of workers concerned (young workers and women are entitled, in certain countries, to longer and more frequent breaks than adult males).

[2] See the Industrial Welfare Society: Shift Work: Current practice in Great Britain, op. cit., pp. 11-12; United Kingdom, Ministry of Labour: Introduction of shift working, A survey (London, HM Stationery Office, 1967); European Economic Community: Le travail dominical dans les Etats membres de la CEE, Etudes, série Politique sociale, No. 17 (Brussels, 1967), and idem: Les salaires dans les branches d'industrie, same series, Nos. 10, 1965, and 12, 1966. Several studies on this subject have been published in the United States, in particular in the Monthly Labor Review (Washington); United States Department of Labor, Bureau of Labor Statistics, Bulletin No. 1142; "Shift provisions in major union contracts, 1958", in Monthly Labor Review, Mar. 1959, and "Provisions for late shifts in manufacturing industries, 1962", ibid., May 1965. Detailed information on shift work rates is published periodically in the bulletin of the Bureau of Labor Statistics. In France, the Federal Republic of Germany and Italy, this information can be found in the collective agreements for the different industries and in works agreements.

In general, financial compensation is different, as already
mentioned, for the different shifts, or for the different days of
the week. Thus the night shift receives a greater compensation
than that received by the evening (or afternoon) shift, and the
latter will receive higher bonuses and allowances than those
received by the morning shift. The last-mentioned shift rarely
receives any compensation; it is considered that it involves less
inconvenience than either of the other two.

Both the fixed amounts and the bonus rates vary considerably
from one country or one industry to another. Thus in the structural
engineering industry, an increase in pay is given, in the Federal
Republic of Germany, only for afternoon or night work; it varies
from 10 to 15 per cent, depending on the region. In the same
industry, the Italian collective agreements provide for a 15 per
cent increase for the same shifts (evening work and night work);
special allowances sometimes specifically to compensate for additional expenditure on food, are added for night work in Italy, as
in other countries. In the French metallurgical industry, certain
regional collective agreements provide that workers employed under
the three-shift system shall receive an additional bonus of a half
an hour's wage, calculated from the prevailing guaranteed rate for
the category concerned; in addition, for a minimum of six hours of
night work (between 10 p.m. and 6 a.m.), an inconvenience bonus
equal to 15 per cent of the effective wage rate is paid. In the
USSR, workers on night shift may receive bonuses ranging from 12 to
30 per cent of the normal wage. Similar provisions can be found
in collective agreements in other countries (Belgium, Netherlands,
United Kingdom).

In the majority of countries and industries, higher rates are
paid for work done on Sundays and public holidays.[1] These rates
are generally in the range of time-and-a-half or double time; but
it is apparently not possible anywhere to combine these special
payments with those for overtime. In any given country, the
supplementary payments may vary considerably. Thus, in France,
they may amount to between 20 and 100 per cent of the normal wage,
in Italy, between 25 and 97 per cent and, in the Federal Republic
of Germany, between 50 and 150 per cent (this latter rate is
generally paid for public holidays).

Whatever the method of calculation, these supplements or
bonuses show the desire of both employers and trade unions (as will
be seen later, such payments are most commonly the subject of
negotiation) to make compensation for the constraints and the
various inconveniences associated with shift work. Nevertheless,
such financial compensation should not lead to an under-estimation
of other forms of compensation, such as a reduction in the hours of
work.[2]

---

[1] The bonuses paid for emergency work done on Sundays or
public holidays will not be considered here; in this case, the
bonuses are usually higher than those for work done periodically at
these times, as is the case with continuous shift work.

[2] This point will be considered again in the section of
Chapter 8 entitled "Bonuses and Allowances".

Information and Consultation

Apart from the standards already mentioned, certain other measures that are not necessarily provided for in national legislation or in collective agreements are of importance in improving the organisation of shift work.

It is necessary, first of all, for the workers to know precisely what their work schedules are, and in particular the starting and stopping times. Several ILO recommendations stress the importance of the posting of notices with regard to work schedules, and especially those of shifts, where shifts are being worked.

Other ILO documents recommend that the competent authority should consult the employers' and workers' organisations on questions relating to hours of work, the ways in which hours of work shall be progressively reduced and shift work.[1] Such negotiations are also provided for in the case of particular branches of industry in order to determine the methods of organisation of shift work (breaks, nightly and weekly rest, frequency of rotation, etc.). Thus the Chemical Industries Committee, in the resolution previously mentioned, adopted in 1952, mentioned several such methods, and stated, inter alia, that "employers should consult workers' organisations on the most suitable systems of shift rotation both from the employers' and workers' point of view".[2] In the United States, many collective agreements (which are normally concluded at the level of the individual undertaking) provide for such procedures; in the same way, in the United Kingdom, the legislation provides for consultation of the workers in the case of any change in the system of work schedules. As will be seen later, shift work is increasingly the subject of negotiations between employers and trade unions and numerous clauses on this subject have been introduced into works agreements and collective agreements.

Welfare

The International Labour Organisation has also emphasised, on several occasions, the need to devote the greatest attention to the health, welfare and safety of the workers when shift work is used, while reducing night work and the disadvantages of this system to a minimum. The recommendations made in this connection are generally linked to the study of technical progress and of automation, and concern both industrial workers and non-manual employees and professional workers. The conclusions adopted by the Coal Mines Committee at its Eighth Session concerning technological improvements and their impact on social conditions in the coal-mining industry state that "the shift rotas should be drawn up ..... after consultation with the workers or their representatives".[3]

---

[1] See, for example, the Reduction of Hours of Work Recommendation, 1962 (No. 116), paragraph 20.

[2] See ILO: Official Bulletin, Vol. XXXV, No. 3, 20 Dec. 1952, p. 200.

[3] See ILO: Official Bulletin, Vol. XLVIII, No. 1, Jan. 1965, p. 90.

The ILO has also drawn attention to the need to organise, for shift workers, welfare facilities designed to meet their special needs - canteens, rest rooms or recreation facilities, transport facilities, etc.[1]

Certain committees have thus called for the provision of hot meals for night shift workers, and of means of transport in addition to public transport, which may be inadequate or non-existent at certain times of day or night, and for adjustments in the operation of welfare facilities in general so as to make them more readily available to shift workers.

A meeting of experts on welfare facilities for industrial workers, held in Geneva in October 1964, came to certain conclusions with regard to the establishment of such facilities, which would in particular meet the needs of shift workers.[2]

Many of the recommendations put forward by the ILO have been included in collective agreements, whether at the level of the undertaking or at a higher level, especially in the English-speaking countries.

Trade Union Policy and Action

As has already been seen, ILO standards and suggestions are the outcome of discussions among the representatives of governments, employers and workers. The recommendations thus arrived at may provide a framework for legislative action; collective agreements, in turn, while fitting into the general context of the legislation, gradually elaborate upon it and thus contribute towards its development.

In view of the importance of the questions raised by shift work, it is desirable that employers and trade unions should hold negotiations on the subject, or at least consultations. It would therefore be of the greatest interest if the position of the trade unions in this connection could be ascertained. Unfortunately, the information available on this subject is scanty and scattered; it can only be hoped that systematic studies will be carried out in this field. At present all that can be done is to note the results of negotiations, the conclusion of works agreements, or special clauses in collective agreements at a higher level. Nevertheless, recent examples of trade union action in this field may be used to illustrate the argument.

What are, first of all, the attitudes of the trade unions with regard to shift work?

The trade unions have given priority to trying to protect certain categories of workers particularly threatened by the inconveniences of shift work, namely children, young people and

---

[1] See Welfare Facilities Recommendation, 1965 (No. 102).

[2] See ILO: Official Bulletin, Vol. XLVII, No. 4, Oct. 1964, pp. 376-390.

women; they have aimed at having night work prohibited for such persons and at limiting their hours of work by providing for daily and weekly periods of rest. In addition, while shift work still seemed to be technically necessary in only a limited number of industries, the trade unions tried to obtain financial compensation that had a dual purpose, namely that of making good the additional expenses associated with this method of working (special bonus for night shifts, bonus for employment under a system of continuous process operation) and that of penalising, as it were, the employer so as to induce him to reduce to a minimum the use of work schedules that were of obvious advantage to him but constituted a constraint for the workers. Financial compensation continued to be the trade unions' main demand as technical and economic considerations made shift work more widespread.

It would seem doubtful whether the trade unions have achieved their objective; although the employer, of course, will take the bonuses and allowances into account in his calculations, he may nevertheless prefer, in certain industries, to pay comparatively high bonuses in order to retain a method of working that has con- siderable financial advantages for the undertaking. The trade unions were gradually forced to realise this and therefore to change their stand in this regard. Thus, while retaining the principle of financial rewards for shift work, the trade unions gradually began to emphasise the improvement of working conditions, and in particular the improved organisation of work schedules or shift rotation and the reduction of hours, with priority for shift workers in any such reduction, which could take the form of addi- tional rest days, longer annual holidays, or even entitlement to earlier retirement. These different trends in trade union action with regard to shift work are reflected in recent publications.

Thus in a report published by the British Trades Union Congress (TUC) on automation and technological change[1], the reduc- tion of hours of work, seen not as a defence against unemployment but as one of the benefits resulting from technical change, is associated with shift work, the increasing use of which is emphasised. The reduction of hours of work is one of the methods suggested for lessening the inconvenience of shift work. Another TUC document, on shift work[2], explains its advantages for employers and emphasises the need to obtain greater advantages for the workers, whether as premiums, bonuses, a reduction in average weekly hours of work, or additional days off; these are to be obtained by negotiation by individual trade unions or federations. The improvement of working conditions is also mentioned - the need to negotiate improvements in the organisation of shift systems (a number of models of shift rotation are suggested), to obtain canteens or slot machines for food and drinks, and transport ser- vices that fit in with the work schedules of the various shifts.

The position adopted by the TUC is reflected in many agreements for different branches of industry. The TUC, while not opposed to the extension of shift work, wants to make sure that the workers

---

[1] Trades Union Congress: Automation and technological change (London, 1965).

[2] Idem: Shift work, Production Memorandum No. 21 (London, 1965).

receive a share in the benefits that accrue, as a result, to the employers and to the economy as a whole. This was the case, for example, in the national agreement for four-shift workers of March 1966 between the employers' federation for the paper and board industry and the unions in the printing, publishing and paper trades. The hours for four-shift continuous work were reduced to an average of 42 per week, while earnings were the equivalent of those for 51 hours, thanks to the supplementary payments introduced. Additional days off were granted on the basis of length of service on shift work.

In the United States, the trade unions have gradually introduced a whole range of rules negotiated as part of plant agreements. These rules are aimed at improving the organisation of shift work and at controlling the operation of the system to the greatest possible extent, so as to protect the workers against unfair practices on the part of the employer. These protection procedures are reflected in a publication of the Department of Labor, which contains more than 120 provisions concerning shift work.[1] These relate, inter alia, to the choice of shift by the worker (permanent day or night shifts are more widely used in the United States than in other countries), such choice being linked to length of service in the undertaking.[2] In addition, any change in the organisation of the shifts must be communicated to the trade union representatives in the undertaking (the way in which shifts are organised will have been negotiated by the union and the management in the first place). This publication is full of suggestions that could usefully provide the basis for negotiations between trade unions and employers in a field where they are still very poorly developed, at least in Europe. Plant agreements, of course, contain a large number of clauses concerning the bonuses granted to the various shifts; the procedures for allotting such bonuses are generally more precise than those found in collective agreements in other countries.

Action taken recently by the trade unions in France should be mentioned, namely the preparation of draft rules and regulations for shift workers, adopted by the chemical workers' federation of the Confédération française démocratique du travail (CFDT). The federation, which is particularly aware of the problems associated with shift work, conducted a survey among the workers that demonstrated the various disadvantages of this method of working.[3] This trade union organisation took the view that the improvement of the conditions of shift workers was not a question of money; to provide financial compensation alone was misleading and inadequate. The position adopted by this trade union resembles

---

[1] United States Department of Labor: Collective bargaining dispositions (hours of work, overtime pay, shift operations) (Washington, Government Printer, 1950).

[2] See Y. Delamotte: Le recours ouvrier dans une entreprise américaine (Paris, A. Colin, 1966), p. 30.

[3] Information on the results of this inquiry and on the draft rules and regulations for shift workers is given in Formation (Paris, CFDT), No. 71, Jan.-Feb. 1967.

that of Dr. Wisner[1], who stated that it was not right to claim, on the worker's behalf, financial compensation for something that was destroying him.[2]

Several of the items in these draft rules and regulations have been taken up in an inter-federation agreement for the chemical industry to which the three main workers' confederations[3] are parties. This draft, which was intended to provide a general framework for use in negotiations between trade unions and employers, contains the provisions described below.

It is suggested that the hours of work of shift workers should be reduced, without any reduction in earnings, to 42 a week, and then to 40, by the grant of an additional rest day every four weeks.

Any worker who works on a public holiday should be given a paid rest day in compensation; this is in addition to the compensation provided for in the collective agreement for working on a public holiday.

For each period of three years of shift work, whether consecutive or not, it should be possible to bring forward the age of retirement by one year, without any reduction in pension.

Before a worker is assigned to shift work, he should first undergo a medical examination (this should cover, in particular, the adjustability of the main functions of the worker's sympathetic nervous system to shift schedules). The physician must inform the worker of the risks associated with shift work, and point out that the worker's health might be seriously affected. Systematic medical examinations every six months must be organised. Transfer to a permanent shift or to day work should be granted on request subject to medical agreement, without loss of earnings.

Shift workers must be given priority in respect of housing, if they so request, under conditions such as to provide the greatest possible confort (sound-proof room for sleep during the day); meals must be served near the workplace in canteens. Publicity drives must be organised in order to make shift workers aware of the hazards associated with their working conditions and to encourage them to take adequate rest.

There should be an automatic return to normal schedules after ten years of shift work or after 50 years of age for any worker who so requests, at a guaranteed rate of pay without downgrading.

---

[1] Professor of Physiology of Work at the Conservatoire des arts et métiers, Paris.

[2] Remarks made at a press conference organised by the Fédération des industries chimiques of the CFDT. See Le Monde (Paris), 1 October 1966.

[3] Confédération française démocratique du travail (CFDT), Confédération générale du travail (CGT), Confédération générale du travail - Force ouvrière (CGT-FO).

Agreement with the employers has already been reached with regard to some of these demands; thus a recent agreement in a chemical undertaking provided for special compensation for public holidays and also contained provisions for early retirement. These allow the worker's age of retirement to be brought forward by a number of years increasing progressively from one year after 15 years of employment under a continuous shift system to five years after 35 years of such employment; in addition, in the event of a transfer for medical reasons, a worker employed under a continuous shift system must receive an increase in wages equal to one-quarter of the bonus for such employment, provided that he is at least 45 years of age and has worked for not less than 25 years under a continuous shift system.[1] Other recent agreements provide for additional paid holidays.

As shift work becomes more widespread and affects branches of economic activity where its introduction meets with resistance, as in offices and departments where the employees, technicians or engineers strongly prefer normal work schedules[2], negotiations between trade unions and employers should contribute to a progressive improvement of the conditions of shift work, since pressure may then be exerted in order to obtain a reduction in hours of work, priority in this respect being given to shift workers.

For example, in the Federal Republic of Germany, thanks to a negotiated reorganisation of shift work, a plan for the reduction of the working week in the iron and steel industry made it possible to reduce the very long hours of work still current in 1957 (53 to 56 hours) to 42 hours in 1966, and then to 40 hours.

The negotiations between employers' and workers' representatives in France, in the iron and steel industry in Lorraine, also led to a reduction in hours of work. Following an agreement of July 1967 on employment problems[3], further agreements concluded in 1968 between the employers' organisations for the iron and steel industry in the Meurthe-et-Moselle and Moselle on the one hand and the trade unions on the other[4] provided that, by the end of 1970, weekly hours of work in departments on continuous operation, which then amounted to 48 hours, would be reduced to 42 hours, as an average over the year.[5]

This reduction would amount, for each worker in a department under continuous operation, to 312 hours of work less each year; he would work on only 39 Sundays, instead of 42, and there would also be a proportionate reduction in work on public holidays; the entitlement to additional paid holidays would not be affected

---

[1] See M. Maurice and C. Monteil: "Le travail continu en équipes successives", in Revue française du travail (Paris), Nos. 3-4, July-Dec. 1964, pp. 3-29.

[2] See ILO Automation and non-manual workers, Labour and Automation Bulletin No. 5 (Geneva, 1967), especially pp. 17-19.

[3] The so-called "Convention sociale".

[4] Confédération générale des cadres, CFDT, CGT and CGT-FO.

[5] See Liaisons sociales (Paris), No. 3357, and Le Monde (Paris), 12 Apr. 1968.

(two days for workers and technicians, three days for supervisors).
The decrease in earnings resulting from this decrease in hours of
work would be made good to the extent of 66 per cent, and even the
true decrease of about 4.6 per cent would be gradually made good by
increases provided for in subsequent agreements on wages, which
were provided for in the same agreement.   These provisions affect
about 23,000 workers, or one-quarter of all those in the iron and
steel industry in Lorraine.   In addition, at Easter and Christmas,
the management will shut down, for three consecutive shifts, all
plant the operation of which can be interrupted without causing
technical difficulties or interfering with the output of the shifts
directly preceding or following the shifts concerned.   The works
committees were extensively consulted before these measures were
applied.

Management Practice

There is no need to repeat here the technical or economic
arguments in favour of shift work.   Clearly an employer, before
he adopts this method of working or extends its use by increasing
the number of shifts or by extending shift work to additional
operations, will tend to consider, in the first place, the economic
interests of the undertaking.   This does not merely involve cal-
culating the advantages of this method of working from the point
of view of productivity;   it also calls for a study of the existing
or potential market in order to be certain that it can absorb the
increased output.   Such a decision must also take other possibilities into account: thus investment in a new factory or workshop may in certain cases turn out to be more profitable than the
introduction of shift work.

Shift work clearly has greater advantages when labour costs
are low in relation to capital charges.   It should also be
remembered that the potential reduction in the capital charges
depends on the type of depreciation or amortisation of the plant
and equipment;   where obsolescence is structural or cyclical in
character, capital costs may be considerably reduced by a more
intensive utilisation of the plant.   Prior study of the labour
market is necessary, therefore, so as to be sure that manpower is
available for the organisation of new shifts;   account must be
taken, in this connection, of the skills required, the location of
this manpower, and the competition on the local market.   The cost
of recruitment must be taken into account, particularly if a period
of training is involved.   In certain cases, shift work may enable
potential manpower to find work: this may be the case with a
section of the female labour force;   such labour would be
attracted by the convenient work schedules, while it would not be
available for full-time work during the day.

Nevertheless, shift work also increases labour costs;   works
agreements and other collective agreements provide for reductions
in the hours of work (paid rest periods, rest days, etc.) and for
the payment of bonuses or allowances.   These will also be
included in the employer's calculations.   Even when due allowance
has been made for these factors, there will still be a number of
problems for the management.

Relative Advantages of Different
Shift Systems for the Employer

Of the various systems of shift work, the employer will have
to choose the type best adapted to his objectives, depending on
the technical and economic position of his undertaking. It will
be remembered that he has three main systems to choose from - the
system of two day shifts, the semi-continuous three-shift system
(with a break at the weekend), and the continuous three-shift
system, without a break at the weekend. Other systems, based on
these three, also exist, such as alternating day and night shifts,
used in particular in the United Kingdom, or systems, such as the
split shift, in which day shifts are supplemented by a shift
working at the end of the day, e.g., from 5 to 10 p.m.[1]

For the employer, the choice between these different systems
is based, in the main, on economic considerations, in which problems of investment, capital and labour costs, the market for the
product and the labour market are all combined. Technical considerations may also be involved, particularly in the case of
products where some degree of continuity in the manufacturing
process is required. The employer will of course also have to
take into account the labour factors mentioned in earlier sections
of this chapter, including the labour legislation in force, particularly in the case of young people and women.

Two-shift systems (two day shifts, or day shift and night
shift) have the advantage of great flexibility. Overtime may be
worked to meet changes in demand or urgent deliveries. Thus, if
two 8-hour shifts are normally worked, their length may, depending
on circumstances, be extended to 10 or 12 hours each. The same
applies to the British system of the alternating day and night
shift. However, several inquiries have shown that this latter
system is not much liked by the workers; this is also true of the
system of two day shifts where more than 8 hours are worked per
shift. When the number of hours worked tends to approximate to
12 hours per shift, an increase in absenteeism, a fall in
productivity or a greater turnover among the work force are sometimes observed.[2]

Three-shift systems, in contrast, impose greater constraints
from the point of view of the organisation of work; a certain
degree of flexibility is possible only with the semi-continuous
system, since maintenance work or emergency repairs can be carried
out during the weekend.

If different weekly hours of work are to be obtained, the
systems of shift rotation described in Chapter III provide suitable
methods; certain systems make it possible to achieve a weekly

---

[1] This latter system is also used in the United Kingdom,
where it is attractive to a certain proportion of the female
labour.

[2] Industrial Welfare Society: Shift work, op. cit.

average of 48 hours, whereas with others 42 hours can be obtained; numerous methods of varying the average weekly hours of work are available.[1]

Whatever the system adopted, however, it must enable each crew to work an identical average weekly number of hours and to earn the same wage. This is one of the main requirements to be met in the organisation of shift work.

Method of Introduction of
Shift Working

Where a new shift work system is to be introduced or adopted for the first time, it is desirable for the employer to consult the workers or their representatives in order to find out their points of view. Several inquiries into shift work have stressed the importance of such consultation (in certain countries, certain plant agreements or collective agreements at a higher level even make this compulsory)[2]; work schedules are also drawn up in the light of the times at which the local transport services operate. Starting times may vary, depending on the way of life in the area concerned.

Employers sometimes introduce shift work when a new factory or workshop is opened; this is clearly a better method, since acquired habits do not have to be changed, and the whole range of problems of work organisation, wages and information and consultation of the workers can be tackled simultaneously. In such a situation, innovation and the testing of new systems of work schedules are possible, with the agreement of the workers.

In contrast, where it is desired to change existing schedules or to change from normal day work to a shift system, resistance to change is generally more frequent. Opposition is based, of course, on the changes in the way of life and on the difficulties associated with shift work; they may also be the consequence of a reduction of overtime on which the workers set great store.[3] The financial advantages of shift work may sometimes be sufficient to overcome the workers' opposition or resistance, but certain employers may then be led to doubt the value of shift work where, after negotiation with the trade unions, they are obliged either to increase

---

[1] Useful information on this subject will be found in the publication already mentioned: "How to plan a shift rota", pp. 19-20 (see also publication No. 140, dated 1966, of the Industrial Society (formerly the Industrial Welfare Society), pp. 21-34).

[2] In the United Kingdom, provisions calling for a secret ballot are contained in the legislation itself. See the Shift System in Factories and Workshops (Consultation of Workpeople) Order, 1936 (No. 1367).

[3] Medical Research Council, Industrial Psychology Research Unit: Problems of shift-working: A review of management opinion (London, Medical Research Council, 1967).

wages or reduce hours of work[1], the more so since the other
advantages of shift work to which the employer can point, such as
free time, are generally less attractive than bonuses or increased
remuneration.

No general solution exists in this field; account must be
taken of the state of the local labour market, and of whether shift
work has been generally adopted in the branch of industry or region
concerned or whether it is the exception.

A number of inquiries have indicated, however, that the choice
of the shift rotation system by the workers or their representatives may facilitate its acceptance.[2] Some firms allow their
workers to choose their work schedules or the type of shift work;
this is possible only where large numbers are employed. It is
desirable that the workers' preferences should be taken into
account to the greatest possible extent, and that it should be
made easy for individuals to change from one schedule or one shift
to another. A certain flexibility or mobility in the composition
of the crews enables many difficulties or tensions among the
various groups of workers to be avoided.[3]

Staff Recruitment and Selection

In the case of shift work, recruitment and selection of staff
are more difficult than in the case of normal schedules. It is
desirable, particularly in the case of continuous working with
night shifts, that any contra-indications should be detected by
means of a suitable medical examination. The factory medical
officer will be able to give useful advice to the workers on the
hazards associated with shift work, on the need for a period of
rest during the day under the best possible conditions, and on
the most suitable foods for the various meals. It will be of
value, in certain cases, to provide for trial periods so that the
adaptability of the individuals concerned can be assessed.[4]

Supervision

One of the difficulties often mentioned in connection with
the introduction of shift work is that of the supervision necessary
for the different shifts. Resistance is sometimes greater among
the supervisory personnel. For this purpose, certain undertakings

---

[1] Medical Research Council: Problems of shift-working, op.
cit., pp. 5-6: "The problem of inducements".

[2] Situations of this type are described in appendix 3 B(a).

[3] Medical Research Council: Problems of shift-working, op.
cit., pp. 11-12: "The flexibility in shift-working arrangements".

[4] See Andlauer and Fourre, op. cit., and Rapport des
VIIes Journées nationales de médecine de travail, Paris, 1962
(Paris, Masson, 1962).

have introduced promotion systems whereby former shift workers or foremen can be promoted to supervisory jobs. The organisation of supervision is sometimes based on a system of overlapping shifts, so that a single supervisor can supervise two different shifts. However, inquiries have shown that in the absence of supervision, particularly during night shifts, the workers have an increased feeling of responsibility, which may contribute to their satisfaction with regard to this method of working.

Communication

Communication or the transmission of instructions and information also gives rise to difficulties. This problem may be solved by the organisation of an overlapping system of supervision covering a variety of shifts. Some undertakings also arrange for log books to be kept; in these log books, the instructions and observations that the supervisor or foreman transmits to his successor, are recorded. Regular meetings of the shift supervisory personnel are sometimes organised during the day, or a system of telephonic communication may make it possible, if special difficulties arise, to contact a member of the management staff at any hour of the day or night. Supervisory personnel may thus, in turn, be obliged to remain at home in order to answer these calls.

The system for the provision of information within the undertaking must be designed in such a way as to reach both the night shifts and the day shifts, and to ensure that from this point of view shift workers are not at a disadvantage. In addition, they must be very clearly informed of the times at which they are on duty and of the periods of rest, so that they can plan the use of their time in advance. Any change in the organisation of their schedules must be made known to them sufficiently in advance for them to be able to make the necessary arrangements.

Welfare Facilities

The organisation of facilities such as canteens, medical services and welfare facilities must also be designed with the shift workers in mind. Some undertakings thus organise canteen services adapted to the shift schedules; hot meals may be specially available during the night. When this is not possible, slot machines may be installed. When the medical or nursing services are unable to operate round the clock, emergency services must be made available to the workers, e.g., first-aid equipment, and steps must be taken to ensure that at least one member of each crew knows how to use it.

Maintenance

Special attention must also be devoted to maintenance, in order to cope with the consequences of the intensive utilisation of plant and machinery. In certain cases it will be necessary to organise maintenance shifts rotating at the same times as the other shifts. In the case of semi-continuous work, maintenance is often done during the weekends, while the maintenance workers take additional days off, in turn, during the week.

CHAPTER VIII

PROVISIONAL ASSESSMENT AND PROSPECTS

If we take an over-all view, man would appear to be struggling, caught up in the machinery governing the productive use of time, for the one thing that gives his existence its true value - the right to use his time as he pleases. For he can achieve this, as the facts show, only at the cost of a constraint on a part of his time - the time spent at work - which also has its value, but of a different kind.[1]

Shift work has emerged, in the course of this study, as providing an outstanding illustration of the economic and social contradictions associated with the development of industrial society: it leads to a distribution of time between hours of work and hours off that demonstrates the conflict in this regard between economic and social requirements, and it expresses in exemplary fashion the gap between the purely chronological concept of time used by both the entrepreneur and the economist, on the basis of considerations of price and cost, and the social concept of time as it is experienced by the workers and which, depending on circumstances, may be a time of self-liberation or of alienation.[2]

From the point of view of the factors leading to its introduction and from that of its effects or consequences, shift work has been looked at as a time pattern corresponding to technical and economic requirements, and involving, both for individuals and for society, a certain number of costs and benefits.[3] (In this connection it is striking that in a society now capable of solving the

---

[1] Translated from the preface by Pierre Naville to the book by Grossin: Le travail et le temps, op. cit., p. viii.

[2] The transition from traditional rural societies to modern urban societies seems to be marked by a change from flexible and complementary uses of time to a rigid timetable and an incompatibility between life at work and away from it. In modern societies there is only apparent flexibility in the use of time, and mechanical requirements are increasingly taking over from social considerations. Thus the fragmentation of job content seems to be matched by a fragmentation of the use of time, both of these features reflecting alienation of man as a worker and as a consumer. See Friedmann, op. cit., p. 195.

[3] If it is accepted that the social sciences do not merely exist to describe or interpret things as they are but must also contribute, in a way, towards defining what they should be - and conversely that the social sciences would be inconceivable in isolation from the economic, political and social context of which they are a part - then the study of shift work falls within the scope of welfare economics and sociology. Two methods of sociological analysis can be envisaged - a functional approach, under which the emphasis is placed on the workers' satisfaction with, and adjustment to, the existing system, and an approach under which priority is given to aims and objectives as compared with means, and one then works one's way back from problems of implementation

(footnote continued on p.94)

multitude of technical and other problems associated with the plac-
ing of space craft on orbit around the earth or its satellites, or
with travelling from the earth to the moon, it has not yet been
possible to express in economic terms what have been known for some
time now as "social costs".)[1]

After the provisional assessment that is being made in the
present concluding part of this study, a number of suggestions will
be put forward with the purpose not of resolving the conflict
between different approaches but of making shift work more acceptable, by answering the question: what is the best way of organising shift work from the point of view of reducing its cost both for
the employer and for the worker, or in other words what is the
optimum pattern of shift work?

The following pages should be read in that light. It is not
claimed that the suggestions or proposals put forward can provide
a general solution to the whole range of problems raised in the
course of this study; clearly in this field there is no single
solution that can be applied in all industries, all sectors of
economic activity, all countries or all regions. The aim is
rather, on the basis of a number of examples, to point out the
direction to be taken by further research that might, in the more
or less distant future, arrive at solutions applicable to particular situations.[2]

Reasons for Shift Work

Whereas originally shift work was largely used to meet technological requirements, particularly in industries in which the
nature of the production process called for continuous operation,
it appears at present to be increasingly the outcome of the economic calculations of the entrepreneur, in the context of the economi
logic of industrial society.

---

[3] (footnote continued from p. 93)

or organisation to those of decision systems, and thereby carries
the analysis to the more political level of the principles that
guide those responsible for the economy and the entrepreneurs.
This latter type of analysis may be thought to bring out more
clearly the conflict between economic and social desiderata, and
thus to provide a theoretical structure for a more fundamental
reconsideration of the use and organisation of shift work.

[1] This was expressed in more or less the same terms by
Floyd C. Mann at the end of "Shift work and the shorter work-week",
p. 124, in Clyde E. Dankert, Floyd C. Mann and Herbert R. Northrup:
Hours of work (New York, Harper and Row, 1965).

[2] There are grounds for thinking that by moving on from fundamental to applied research, it will be possible to advance, at one
and the same time, the study of certain branches of the social
sciences and the analysis of the problems facing the people responsible for charting the course of economic and social development.

Historically, this method of working became more widespread
when entrepreneurs realised that, by operating machines or installations for longer than the normal hours of work, they could divide
up the cost of their capital investment among a larger number of
units of output, thereby reducing costs and correspondingly increasing profits.[1]

As technology becomes more complex, thanks to the progress of
science, new investments become necessary, and this leads to a more
intensive use of machinery and plant 24 hours a day and seven days
a week.   This economic factor accounts for the fact that day and
night shifts are found in undertakings where technology does not
require continuous operation, as in the iron and steel industry,
the chemical industry, and the paper and board industry.[2]   Shift
work has also been used, in recent decades, in the data-processing
industry, since computers are very expensive, even when leased, and
very rapidly become technically outdated.

This method of working, however, is also in use in industries
in which machines or products become particularly rapidly obsolescent
- the automobile industry and the electrical or electronics industry.
In all these industries, the cost of investment in capital, as compared with the cost of labour, is such as to encourage intensive
operation of plant.   The progress of automation was expected
gradually to reduce the amount of labour employed both in offices
and in workshops, but in fact even non-manual employees, technicians
and managers are now required to do shift work, both in the day
time and at night.

Future Development

How will shift work develop in the future, as far as this can
be foreseen more or less in the long term?   The first question
that arises is whether the number of manual and non-manual workers
obliged to accept this method of working will continue to increase
in the future, as the trend observed over the last ten years (particularly in France, Japan and the United Kingdom) would appear to
show.   It is difficult, of course, to give any precise answers in
this connection.   Nevertheless, theories based solely on economic
calculations show that in many cases[3] the gains obtained by the use
of shift work are markedly greater than the additional cost of the
bonuses paid to the workers, the increased wear and tear of the
machinery or the decrease in productivity at certain times of the

---

[1] See Mott, Mann, McLoughlin and Warwick, op. cit., p. 31.
For an explanation of the concept of optimum pattern of shift work,
see M. Kabaj: Problems of shift work as a means of improving
capacity utilisation (Vienna, United Nations Industrial Development
Organisation, 1969).   That document was intended for a meeting of
experts held in Rio de Janeiro in March 1969.

[2] Floyd C. Mann: "Shiftwork and the shorter workweek",
op. cit.

[3] Certain economists, for example Marris, op. cit., have
expressed doubts in this connection.   See above, Chapter II.

day. In addition, everything points to the conclusion that the
increasing rate at which equipment and products become obsolescent
will help to promote the extension of shift work. This does not
necessarily mean, of course, that the numbers of workers on shift
work will continue to rise: it is possible that shift work may be
used more in branches of economic activity or branches of industry
where automation will gradually tend to reduce the numbers employed.
In addition, it is not certain that automation, by itself, tends to
promote the extension of shift work: recent research has shown that
there is no link between the extent of automation of an undertaking
and the frequency with which shift work is used[1]; in certain cases,
automation of the production process has been found to reduce the
number of shifts previously required with more traditional techniques, and the use of increasingly modern machines does not necessarily lead to a more frequent recourse to shift work.[2] More
detailed studies will be necessary, capable of distinguishing
between what is due, in the use of shift work, to technical constraints or economic considerations and between cases in which the
only possible production process requires shift work and cases in
which non-continuous processes are available. It must also be
remembered that economic factors are not the only ones to affect
the decision of the entrepreneur in this connection: in certain
cases he may be led to adopt shift work because of the location of
the undertaking, or because it is impossible to enlarge on the spot
or to decentralise; moreover some industries are seasonal, and
commercial considerations or considerations relating to the state
of the market may also come into play.

Whatever the reasons that lead him to use shift work, the
entrepreneur, while taking into account the legislation in force,
will have to cope with manpower, supervision, management and personnel policy problems, as well as with the resistance of certain
categories of workers who prefer work schedules which they correctly
consider to be more propitious to a normal way of life.[3] Thus, all
forecasting in this field must take into account not only the
economic aspects of shift work but also its social or labour aspects.

---

[1] Naville: L'automation et le travail humain, op. cit.,
p. 236 (quoted by Grossin, Le travail et le temps, op. cit., p. 101).

[2] Grossin, ibid., pp. 98-99; see also Lucas, op. cit., p. 252.

[3] Grossin states (Le travail et le temps, op. cit., p. 104)
that plant managers can fairly easily find unskilled workers for
shift work, but have greater difficulty in finding skilled workers,
and still greater difficulty in finding technicians and supervisors.
He points out that above a certain standard of living what people
come to want is not so much increased earnings as a "normal" working life, and he considers that resistance to the three-shift
system may be expected to increase. In the same way, H.A. Rhee
comments that the idea of working on the night or evening shifts,
and especially of working an alternating shift, is considered as a
threat to the status of the office worker, who strongly prefers the
9 to 5 routine, five days a week. See his Office automation in
social perspective: The progress and social implications of electronic data processing (Oxford, Blackwell, 1968).

Pros and Cons of Various Systems for
the Workers

The consequences for the workers of this method of working
must therefore be considered afresh. It has already been stressed
in preceding chapters that not enough social research has been done
in this field, although a good deal of material has been published
on certain aspects of shift work, particularly on its physiological
effects. While the detailed findings concerning the effects of
this method of working on the various aspects of the worker's life
- physical and mental health, family life, social life - will not
be repeated here, the gist of the main findings will be recalled,
and greater emphasis placed on the conditions leading to the
appearance of the disorders and disturbances observed in these
various respects. The marked interdependence between the various
aspects and effects of shift work is bound to spring to notice
immediately and to remind readers who might have forgotten it of
the underlying unity of the physical and mental functions of the
human body, as well as of the closeness of the relationship between
man and his social environment and between working life and life
away from work.[1]

The various systems of shift work in use do not all have the
same disadvantages. In addition to systems involving shift rotation, which are the commonest, there are permanent day and night
shifts. The latter cause less disturbances than the former, particularly from the physiological point of view.

Thus a worker on the morning shift (for example, from 6 a.m.
to 2 p.m., or from 5 a.m. to 1 p.m. is able, if not to have a
normal family life, at least to be present for the evening meal and
to participate in family or social activities in the evenings.
Several inquiries have shown, in fact, the workers' preference for
the morning shift; it gives more time off and a more or less
normal amount of sleep.

From a social point of view, the afternoon shift (from 1 or
2 p.m. to 9 or 10 p.m.) has the greatest over-all disadvantages,
especially for families where the children are still young: the
worker on the afternoon shift is in fact at home when the children
are not, and vice versa. The major activities of the day, both
family and social, generally take place in the evening. One of
the few advantages of the afternoon shift, which is appreciated by
certain workers, is the fact that they do not have to get up very
early and, in the case of women, that they can do their housework
and shopping in the morning, like the majority of women who do not
go out to work.

As far as the night shift is concerned (from 9 or 10 p.m. to
5 or 6 a.m.), its disadvantages are so marked as to deserve
emphasis. The most important is obviously physiological in
character - the problem of the inversion of the circadian rhythm
previously mentioned; but the disadvantages from the point of view

---

[1] In this sense, the shift worker is a product of industrial
society and of the logic on which it is based; clearly, therefore,
solutions to the problems with which he is confronted must be
sought essentially in social structures and the aims that they
reflect.

of family life are by no means insignificant. Relations between
the spouses are obviously made difficult, especially if both are
working. On the other hand, this shift does give time off during
the day, but if that time is used for a second paid job, is there
any real advantage? It must be remembered, however, that a
minority of workers, after having tried it, prefer night work
(they are generally unmarried or married without children): they
appreciate, in addition to the bonuses, which are sometimes attractive, the atmosphere of night work, and in particular the absence
of supervision, the team spirit, and the feeling of greater freedom and increased responsibility.

Although both have disadvantages as well as advantages, permanent shifts seem preferable to rotating shifts. In addition,
inquiries conducted among workers operating these different systems
have shown that the majority, in both cases, prefer the permanent
shift system.[1]

Nevertheless, as has already been seen, the system most
commonly used in the majority of countries is that involving shift
rotation, although it has the greatest disadvantages, especially
in the case of the three-shift system. Weekly rotation, which is
the commonest, implies a change of rhythms and habits each week,
and thus cancels out the whole range of advantages and disadvantages
specific to each shift. To this must be added the difficulty for
friends and relations of foreseeing which days or weeks will be the
most suitable; it is for this reason that the worker on a rotating
shift system feels himself, or is felt by others, to be living on
the margin of society.[2] In addition, while the worker on a permanent shift has an opportunity, in certain cases, to change shift[3],
this opportunity does not exist in the case of rotating shifts.
The only possible alternative is to change over to normal day work,
if this is available, but this change generally involves a loss of
earnings.

Possible Improvements

The real or potential disadvantages of shift work are sufficiently
well recognised for attempts to be made to reduce them to the
greatest possible extent. It is necessary to take into account
not only the economic advantages of continuous operation of the
machines but also the social cost of continuous work by workers
employed alternately during the day and at night, in order to

---

[1] See Mott, Mann, McLoughlin and Warwick, op. cit., p. 303,
and Maurice and Monteil: Vie quotidienne et horaires de travail,
op. cit., p. 106.

[2] It is understandable, therefore, that those inclined towards
active social participation, thanks to their level of education or
of skill, or out of personal interest, will be particularly dissatisfied with the rotating shift system.

[3] In the United States, where this system appears to be commoner than elsewhere, seniority in the undertaking enables the
worker to choose his shift; this is even laid down in plant agreements.

determine the best solutions both for the individuals concerned and for society. Measures of two kinds may be considered for this purpose, the first tending to achieve the best arrangement of existing systems, and the second establishing new working conditions so as to minimise the social cost of shift work.

Up to the present, emphasis has been placed mainly on measures of the first type: the improvement of the systems already in use, the search for schedules causing the least disturbance to the workers, and methods of facilitating their adjustment and the preservation of family and social life. Yet in view of the disadvantages summed up in the previous section, why are rotating shift systems, in particular, still so prevalent? Mott, Mann, McLoughlin and Warwick, in the publication already mentioned, point out that studies carried out by management have shown that the rotating shift system is less expensive than the permanent shift system because it requires fewer workers to man the same number of work stations.[1] But the size of the savings in labour costs is not clear and, in any case, it is not clear that such savings can compensate for the social costs associated with rotating shifts, although up to the present no study has evolved a method of measuring and weighing such costs so that they can be introduced into an accounting system.[2]

Another explanation is provided by the preference of the workers, in practice, for the system that they are already operating, whatever the preferences expressed verbally in the course of opinion surveys; once they have become used to a system, the workers fear change of any kind. Weekly shift rotation would appear, in essence, to be a compromise; advantages and disadvantages are balanced, and both employers and workers are apparently satisfied; like many compromises, however, it is an obstacle to improvement. It is not enough merely to record feelings of dissatisfaction, or even desires for improvement, in order to initiate a change. Even if it is assumed that the employer is favourably disposed towards a change in the shift system (he would have to be, or no change would be possible), other requirements need to be met before such a change can be made in the best interests of the workers.

In any event, measures to minimise the social cost of shift work, which have already been described, deserve greater attention. In particular, a decrease in hours of work can open up new possibilities for the use of shift work. There is general agreement that this is so.[3] The adoption of shift work enables plant and equipment to be used more intensively and may, under certain conditions, increase productivity; a decrease in hours of work can permit a

---

[1] Mott, et al., op. cit., pp. 308-309.

[2] This might be an interesting case for the development of a social indicator in the context of welfare economics.

[3] In Norway a marked extension of shift work has been observed since hours of work were reduced in 1959; this has also been noted in certain branches of economic activity in the Federal Republic of Germany.

more efficient organisation of shift work[1], by making it possible to
reduce the length of the shifts (six-hour shifts instead of eight-
hour shifts, for example), by freeing a greater number of rest days
and Sundays during the cycle of rotation, or by reducing the number
of night shifts worked by any one person. The difficulties at
present involved in the choice between rotating and permanent
shifts would be lessened if the hours worked on each shift were reduced and the number of rest days increased.

The very numerous suggestions or proposals made by writers on
shift work need to be reviewed, and further consideration given to
those that appear most suitable, in the light of the various aspects
of this method of working; the best solutions are, of course, those
whereby costs can be kept or reduced to a minimum, at one and the
same time, for the employer, the workers, and society as a whole.[2]

Work Schedules

Starting with the shift systems most commonly used and with
those that give rise to the greatest number of difficulties (in
other words, three-shift systems involving a night shift)[3], consideration will first be given to the question of the optimum spacing of
the shifts over the day, and then the optimum rhythm of shift
succession, with or without rotation.

The spacing of the shifts over the day, and the starting and
finishing times for each shift, depend, in principle, on the number
of hours worked by each shift. In general, at least for the three-
shift system, as is well known, each of the three shifts lasts
8 hours; the timing of these shifts may vary, the morning shift
most commonly starting around 6 a.m. in urban areas, but sometimes
a little earlier (4 or 5 a.m.) in rural areas.[4]

Nevertheless, if it is assumed that the three shifts each last
8 hours, the starting time of the morning shift may be later or
earlier; if it is later (e.g. with an 8 a.m. - 4 p.m. - 12 midnight,
or 7 a.m. - 3 p.m. - 11 p.m. timetable), the schedules will give
better conditions for sleep and for rest during the day; if the
starting time is earlier (e.g. 4 a.m. - 12 noon - 8 p.m., or 3 a.m.
- 11 a.m. - 7 p.m.), the schedules fit in with the times of the main

---

[1] Technical progress, particularly automation, to the extent
that it enables hours of work to be reduced, may tend to slow down
the extension of shift work, although in the short run it tends
rather to promote its extension, at least in certain branches of
economic activity.

[2] Consideration will be given here to the proposals of a number
of authors, especially Mott, Mann, McLoughlin and Warwick; Maurice
and Monteil, and Andlauer and Fourre, and in the following publications: United Kingdom, Ministry of Labour: Introduction of shift
working, op. cit., and J.H. Downie: Some social and industrial
implications of shift work (London, Industrial Welfare Society,
1963).

[3] Most of the suggestions made apply also to two-shift working
or to similar systems.

[4] This gives the following schedules: 6 a.m. - 2 p.m. - 10 p.m.,
or 4 a.m. - 12 noon - 8 p.m.

meals, and a long period of rest during the day, after the night shift, is possible. In addition, the starting time of the morning shift may coincide with the minimum of the curve of central temperature (which is usually located between 2 and 3 a.m.), thus following, as certain physiologists would wish, the circadian rhythm. The adoption of such schedules, of course, is possible only if the undertaking can solve the problems associated with the transport of the workers; in addition, the schedules must take into account to the greatest possible extent the local way of life. Since any solution involves an attempt to reconcile, at one and the same time, the requirements of sleep, daytime rest, and family life, the workers concerned must obviously be consulted; with their agreement, trial periods can also be considered.

While the principle of eight hours of duration for each shift is widely accepted, since the majority of workers prefer a shorter working week rather than a working day of less than eight hours, inquiries have nevertheless reported cases in which the number of hours worked by the night shift is either more or less than eight. If it is shorter (for example, seven hours), the aim is to make this shift less objectionable; if it is longer than eight hours the aim is to avoid clashes with meal times, or to provide better conditions for daytime sleep or for family life, by correspondingly reducing the hours worked by the day shifts. This is one possible opportunity for change; further studies might be able to demonstrate the advantages of a solution of this type.[1]

Another suggestion might be adopted, namely that of the organisation of shifts working six or seven hours a day. A system could be organised, for example, consisting of four shifts (rotating or permanent) each working for six hours, or of five or six shifts each working six or seven hours; this would give a working week of 36, 35 or even 30 hours, the last figure corresponding, of course, to a marked reduction in the weekly hours of work. Some of the disadvantages already pointed out could be reduced or even eliminated by such arrangements. By adjusting the schedules, it would thus be possible either to increase the likelihood that the worker would be present at the main family meals (for example with the following schedule: 6 a.m., 12 noon, 6 p.m., 12 midnight), or to follow more closely the circadian rhythms so as to provide better conditions for daytime sleep (for example with the schedule 2 a.m., 8 a.m., 2 p.m., 8 p.m.). Although some inquiries have shown that the workers prefer an eight-hour day and a five-day week, the schedules just described might well be approved if they were associated with a reduction in the hours of work, shift workers being given preference in this connection. It may perhaps be objected that a six-hour day (or night) might encourage double-jobbing, but this problem, however important it may be, is not peculiar to shift work. It will, of course, become more acute as hours of work are reduced, but it is, nevertheless, a problem in its own right, linked with the way of life or the logic of industrial

---

[1] Grossin, in Le travail et le temps, op. cit., pp. 88-93, states that according to an inquiry conducted in 1961 in the engineering and electrical industries, the hours of work of particular shifts under the three-shift system were often different; many night shifts worked for more than eight hours.

society.[1]   Shift workers could be warned of the health hazards of
doing more than one job.[2]

Shift Rotation or Permanent Shifts

While shift rotation - a compromise for both the employer and
the workers - is commonly used, permanent shifts, in principle, have
major advantages, as has already been pointed out. Studies,
particularly medical studies, conducted mainly in the Federal
Republic of Germany, United Kingdom and the United States are
already available that reach conclusions favourable to permanent
shifts, especially in the case of the night shift.[3] In addition,
the doubts or fears sometimes expressed in this connection by the
workers could be overcome if they were given the opportunity, if
not to choose their shift when they were engaged, at least to
change shift after a few years of service, as is the practice, for
example, in the United States.

Night work should, as far as possible, be kept for volunteers,
who would periodically undergo medical examinations in order to
check their adjustment to daytime sleep, account being taken of
their family situation and housing conditions.

If, however, after more thorough investigations, the principle
of shift rotation were retained, what would be the preferred solution
with regard to the frequency of rotation?

This question is still highly controversial; while a weekly
frequency (five, six or seven days) is the commonest - a compromise
solution that also corresponds to a social norm, namely the seven-
day length of the week - opinion is still divided between a rapid
shift rotation or, on the contrary, a lengthening of the cycle of
rotation.

---

[1] See H. L. Wilensky: "The moonlighter", in Industrial
Relations (Berkeley, California), Vol. 3, No. 1, Oct. 1963. This
author states that one of the determining factors in moonlighting
is the flexibility and the deviant character of the work schedules
in comparison with the usual schedules.

[2] W. L. Gimberg and R. Bergman state, on the basis of a study
on the use of six-hour shifts in an undertaning where the working
week had been reduced to 36 hours, that absenteeism was higher
among workers doing a second job. Many workers, in fact, had made
use of their time off to take a second job ("Workers' attitudes
toward shorter hours", in Monthly Labor Review (Washington),
Vol. LXXIX, No. 11, Nov. 1956, pp. 1268-1270).

[3] Mention may be made here of the important study by E. Ulich:
Zur Frage der Schicht- und Nachtarbeit bei Dreischicht- und
Vierschichtarbeiten, op. cit. Floyd C. Mann also recommends
permanent shifts; according to his analysis of the advantages and
disadvantages of the different shift systems studied, permanent
shifts appeared to be more conducive to the wellbeing of the worker
than rotating shifts. ("Shift work and the shorter workweek",
op. cit., p. 123.)

What are, in the first place, the arguments in favour of a rapid rotation, i.e., one in which the shifts rotate every two or three days? It is considered, in this case, that it is preferable to restrict the period spent on the night shift, which is believed to be the most harmful, and in general the shift least readily accepted by the workers. In addition, with a rapid shift rotation, it is believed that adjustment problems and their associated disorders will be eliminated or at least reduced.[1] Studies from which definite conclusions can be reached are still few in number, but it is also true that resistance to the use of rapid rotation has been based, up to the present, only on intuition or arguments of disputed value.

Long periods (i.e., longer than a week) between shift changes are most often favoured by writers on the subject; such periods, varying in length from a fortnight to a month or even longer, are, it will be remembered, more commonly used in the United Kingdom and the United States than in other countries. The arguments in their favour are based on the possibility that these systems provide of a better adjustment of the sympathetic nervous system to changes in schedule. The regularity of family and social life, and the greater ease of planning social activities and contacts in advance, are also stressed. The major disadvantage, however, is the longer period spent on the night shift.

The use of intermediate solutions, such as weekly rotation or similar systems, has been encouraged by the absence of any decisive arguments in favour of either of the preceding systems. In support of intermediate systems, emphasis is placed on the accumulation of fatigue or the decreased output sometimes observed in the case of long periods between shift changes; the cumulative effects of the disadvantages linked with a particular shift can be reduced by weekly rotation. The opinions of the workers would seem to be in agreement with this: "One week on nights is quite enough; a longer period would be too tiring". As is well known, however, the workers perfer the system that they are used to; whatever the arrangement under consideration, habit constitutes a kind of adjustment.[2] Proposals based on more thorough physiological studies might receive the workers' approval if they were adequately informed of the results, and if new forms of organisation were tried out with their approval over a sufficiently long period. In this field, there is a risk that habit may too often be a means of defence against all possibility of change.

Weekly rotation does have the support of the workers, no doubt because it is the most common arrangement. A short cycle of rotation appears to be in conflict with the pace of their lives: "There wouldn't be time to get used to it.". Between this evil and the possibility of being assigned for a long period to one of the shifts that they dislike (the night shift or the afternoon shift), the workers prefer the intermediate solution.

---

[1] See, in particular, P. Andlauer and L. Fourre: "Etude de la nuisance comparée de deux modalités d'alternance", in _Revue française du travail_ (Paris, Ministère du Travail), Oct.-Dec. 1965, pp. 35-50. This study tends to prove that rapid rotation is preferable to weekly rotation.

[2] See P. Andlauer and L. Fourre: _Aspects ergonomiques du travail en équipes alternantes,_ op. cit., pp. 113-114. Many of the proposals put forward here have been taken from this excellent literature survey.

Two original solutions may be mentioned here, namely the work schedules used on the German railways and those associated with the 25-hour day.[1] The first involves the organisation, for each working place, of a number of shifts whose schedules change nearly every day, periods of rest varying from 12 to 60 hours and being proportionate to the number of hours worked. Such a system, however, is not suitable for all types of work. Those of railway workers can be reconciled, in certain cases, with prolonged periods at work (more than 8 hours), where the workload is smaller than in other occupations. The diversity of the tasks to be performed in this case, is an incentive to the introduction of more highly differentiated and flexible arrangements than would be possible in industry.

The 25-hour day, suggested by Eränkö, has never been tried out; it is based on a gradual displacement of the work schedules, and may promote, in this way, a gradual adjustment to change. The length of each shift would then be 8 hours and 20 minutes, complete inversion of the circadian rhythms being achieved after 25 days. Numerous objections could be made, however, to this solution; in particular, it makes participation in family or social life more difficult, since the continual changes in schedule make it impossible to plan in advance with any degree of precision.

These two examples, in spite of their imperfections, do have the merit of pointing the way towards new solutions, and demonstrate that innovation is possible in this field.

As we have seen, the selection of work schedules and the determination of the number of hours to be worked per day by the different shifts are certainly of importance from the point of view of family or social life, or from that of the quality of rest, but the choice between shift rotation and permanent shifts is even more difficult and raises even more questions, to most of which, in any case, no answer has been found. For this reason, the hope must once again be expressed that research, if possible interdisciplinary, will be carried out that will provide, if not ready-made solutions that can be generally applied, at least reliable information for those who will have,[2] in the future, to take the responsibility for making such choices.

---

[1] See Publications du XIIe Congrès international de médecine du travail, Helsinki, 1-6 juillet 1957 (Helsinki, 1958), Vol. III: Travaux, papers by K.H. Schunk, pp. 131-134, and Olavi Eränkö, pp. 134-135.

[2] It should be mentioned here that, according to Floyd C. Mann (Mott, Mann, McLoughlin and Warwick, op. cit., pp. 314-315), long-term studies would be necessary to separate out the cause and effect relationships among the hypotheses generally formulated. Special research on the ability of the workers to adjust to variations in circadian rhythms would be desirable; nevertheless, greater account should be taken of the effects of the environment. More systematic research should be considered with regard to shift rotation and permanent shifts, and to the frequency of rotation; these studies should take into consideration other social variables.

Individual Adjustment and Selection
for Shift Work

We have seen that, with present shift rotation systems, major
problems of physiological and psychological adjustment arise.
The question then arises of the possibility of selecting people for
shift work on the basis of their adaptability.

Pointing out that these two kinds of adjustment, namely
physiological and psychological, are doubtless not independent of
one another, Andlauer and Fourre concluded that the current state
of knowledge was not such as to enable valid rules to be put forward
for predicting adaptability to the changes in work schedules
associated with the three-shift system.[1] All that is possible,
therefore, is what might be described as an intuitive method of
medical selection. According to certain studies, undertakings
avoid assigning to work under the three-shift system any worker who
has undergone a major surgical operation, or any worker suffering
from neurological disease, from a serious pathological disorder,
or from a confirmed gastric or duodenal ulcer. Such selection
criteria are mentioned among the conclusions of physiological or
medical studies (Thiis-Evensen, Burger, etc.) that stress the need
for a pre-employment medical examination; other writers also
mention the so-called psychosomatic disorders as a contra-indication
to work under the three-shift system. All are agreed that continuous shift work should not be done by workers over 50 years of
age (if they have never done shift work) or by young people
under 18 years of age (this is the lower statutory limit in the
majority of countries).

Another important aspect of industrial medicine is the
prevention of disease and the protection of the workers even before
it is possible to detect any pathological disorder. A number of
authors stress the need for periodic examinations adapted to the
situation of shift workers and each including, in particular, a
long conversation with the individual worker. During these
conversations, information should be sought on any use of stimulants
or tranquilisers, the consumption of which, it is believed, is
particularly high among shift workers, or those shift workers who
regularly do night work. Advice could be given, on this occasion,
on the prevention of common disorders of the digestive or
sympathetic nervous system.

A question often raised, in the context of industrial medicine,
is that of transfers. Transfer from a three-shift system to normal
day work gives rise, in addition to the difficulties associated with
any transfer, to that of the loss of the financial advantages
associated with shift work. The industrial medical officer must
in all cases carefully assess the need for a transfer: Andlauer
and Fourre point out[2] that the same minor disorders occurring,
on the one hand, in a worker who dislikes the system, and on the
other, in a worker who likes it for various reasons, may not have
the same significance, and should doubtless not lead to the same
decisions.

---

[1] Andlauer and Fourre: _Aspects ergonomiques du travail en
équipes alternantes_, op. cit., p. 126.

[2] Ibid., p. 132.

Information and Community
Facilities

The difficulties to which the three-shift system gives rise
are not all of a kind. Provided that he is given adequate information, some difficulties can be overcome if the worker makes an
effort to adjust. Advice can be given to shift workers on such
things as the timing and the composition of meals, or the conditions
appropriate to rest or sleep. This is one of the tasks of works
welfare services or medical services. Since eating habits are not
very easy to change, explanatory information must be given to
the workers to encourage them to respect certain dietetic principles.
It has been suggested, for example, that eating habits should be
completely reversed when the worker is on the night shift: a light
meal should be eaten in the evening before work is started, followed
by a full meal around midnight, and another full meal on coming off
night shift, followed in turn by a long period of relaxation and
leisure before sleep, which should continue until the evening. Such
an arrangement would of course involve a complete upsetting of
habits but deserves to be tried out, if only on an experimental
basis, in an entire undertaking, over a long period. Facilities
such as works canteens should enable shift workers, whatever their
shift, to eat one of their main meals in the plant.

The fewer opportunities for rest are also one of the difficulties of shift work. Here again, a policy of providing advice
and information is necessary so that the attention of the workers
can be drawn to the need for an average amount of sleep, by explain-
ing to them the problems raised by the inversion of sleep rhythms.
Some undertakings, for example, have organised film shows or talks
on the various aspects of shift work, followed by discussions in
which the workers were given the opportunity to ask questions and
to make suggestions themselves.

Certain writers recommend that in housing constructed in
industrial areas the architect should provide for at least one
sound-proofed room in each flat (the aim should, of course, be
increasingly to construct dwellings that are completely sound-
proof), using tried and tested techniques. This would certainly
be desirable and would reduce interference with rest, without
waiting for the provision - probably still in the distant future -
of fully satisfactory urban living conditions for the workers.
In addition, attempts must be made to reduce the time spent in
travelling between the home and the place of work, and to improve
transport facilities, so as to avoid additional fatigue for the
workers, particularly for those on shift work.

Certain community facilities must also be provided, to reduce
the shift worker's feeling of isolation, or of living on the margin
of society. A better adjustment to shift work has often been
found in communities where the majority of the population was
engaged in this method of working. In such situations, the time
pattern of local social life is itself arranged in the light of
the predominant work schedules. In all cases, however, it is
possible to imagine an organisationsl policy for leisure activites
that would be better adapted to continuous shift work. Local
authorities, works committees and local voluntary bodies would
then have to take steps to ensure that the scheduling of certain
cultural and leisure activities was arranged in the light of the
hours of shift workers, wherever they constitute an appreciable
proportion of the working population.

Bonuses and Allowances

As is well known, the trade unions, in trying to limit the
spread of shift work, have been able to induce employers to pay
bonuses and allowances for such work. These supplementary payments are intended, at one and the same time, to impose a kind of
penalty on the employer and to compensate the worker for the
additional expense (transport, meals, snacks, etc.) or for the
disadvantages or inconvenience of this method of working. Employers
have generally preferred to accept such conditions, sometimes after
a strike, than to negotiate with the trade unions over the organisation of shift work itself.[1]

Nevertheless, it may be asked whether the system of compensatory payments does not constitute an obstacle to the improvement
of the organisation of shift work. Certain workers may be induced
to take up work on rotating shifts, or on permanent night shift, in
order to obtain the bonuses and allowances associated with these
methods of working. These are often workers who are in difficulties
and their financial gain will not counterbalance by far the
resulting social cost. The preference of the workers for certain
systems of shift rotation or to certain shifts for financial
reasons may thus constitute an obstacle to change.

As already pointed out, trade unionists now consider that
trade union action in this field must be directed to new objectives
- a reduction in hours of work, opportunities for workers to return
to normal day work after a number of years and without loss of
earnings, the negotiation of new work schedules and early retirement are all possibilities worth exploring.

The financial advantages that have been won must not, of
course, be lost as a result, but could be gradually incorporated
in the wage (and thereby cease to be regarded as supplementary
payments) as other benefits, not financial in character, were
obtained. Such benefits might perhaps constitute a more effective
brake on the extension of shift work and, for the workers, would
be a better form of compensation for the inconvenience and constraints associated with this method of working.

Advantage of Shift Work for a Developing Economy

In the so-called under-developed countries, capital is scarce
and is not enough to provide employment for the entire available
working population, the greatest proportion of which is engaged in
agriculture, where productivity is low.

---

[1] It is noteworthy that both in the United States and in France,
the resistance of employers to the carrying out of sociological
inquiries among shift workers has been based on the same arguments
that the workers, in their answers, will stress the disadvantages
of shift work, and that the trade unions will take advantage of
these results to demand increased bonuses. (Mott, Mann, McLoughlin
and Warwick, op. cit., p. 310). The author of the present report
had the same experience in carrying out his inquiry (Vie quotidienne
et horaires de travail, op. cit.).

In many cases the aim is to switch labour as rapidly as possible from agriculture to industry. The speed at which that can be done is limited by the availability of the social and industrial capital required to provide housing and public services for the workers thus transferred, and by the availability of skilled workers and of technical, supervisory and managerial staff.

If capital imports are neglected, the rate of growth of the stock of capital depends on the proportion of the national income saved, hourly productivity in the capital goods industries and the number of hours spent in productive work per year. If the last two of these factors are fixed, only an increase in savings can lead to a faster rate of growth, which presupposes a reduction in current consumption in order to obtain an increase in employment.

The rate of utilisation of capital could also be increased by the adoption of a shift system. This could lead to inconvenience for a section of the population, but the alternative before them is not so much day work or night work as night work or no work at all.

This argument, put forward by R. Marris[1], presupposes the existence of a sufficiently developed industrialised sector. It also presupposes that the increase in the output of the industries concerned will be in step with the home or foreign market. If this problem is put on one side, shift work in the developing countries has two advantages: it makes it possible to decrease the scarcity of capital, in the sense that, in the initial stages, output will be increased without any great increase in the demand for capital goods; and the resulting income and savings will make possible, in a later stage, an increased demand for capital. Nevertheless, these effects will not really help to promote development unless they are associated with transmission or diffusion effects in the economy.

It should be remembered, in addition, that the shortage of skilled labour and other qualified personnel may result in a lower labour productivity. The organisation of shift work should serve as an incentive to efforts in the field of manpower training.

It should also be pointed out that the abundance of labour (or at least of unskilled labour) and the scarcity of capital, although not exactly reflected by cost ratios, should lead to a combination of these factors such that capital is used as intensively as possible, even if the number of workers who have to be employed is excessive by the standards of developed countries.

---

[1] Marris, op. cit., pp. 12-14.

APPENDICES

1. Case Studies on the Reasons for the
    Adoption or Extension of Shift
    Work

    In order to illustrate the reasons that may induce an under-
taking to adopt or extend shift work, the industries and sectors
of economic activity in which this method of working is mainly
used will be considered, namely, the metal industry, the automobile industry, general engineering, the chemical industry, the
petroleum industry, the lime and cement industry, the textile
industry (both natural and synthetic fibres), the paper and board
industry, the glass industry, the sugar industry, and establishments
using electronic data processing equipment (computers). These case
studies, for the most part, have been extracted from inquiries
conducted for employers' and workers' organisations[1], or from the
publications of these organisations.

Metal Fabrication

    In this sector of economic activity, particularly in the iron
and steel industry, the operation of blast furnaces has traditionally required the organisation of successive shifts for technical
reasons that are easy to understand. Nevertheless, in view of the
diversity of the operations and techniques used in this industry,
it is necessary to distinguish between occasional recourse to shift
work and the permanent use of this method of working.

    Shift work may be used from time to time, usually as a means
of dealing with a rush of work. Certain machines, for example, may
have to be operated more intensively, and a second shift may be
organised if the overtime worked by the first is not sufficient.
This presupposes, of course, that the necessary manpower is available,
either as a result of the recruitment of temporary workers or by the
transfer of labour from one plant to another. In this case, therefore, two shifts are used, working for a varying number of hours,
but both on day work.

    Shift work may, in contrast, be permanent in character; this
is generally the case in the iron and steel industry. Here, too,
however, a number of different situations may be found, depending
on the severity of the constraints imposed by technical or
economic factors. Thus, while continuous operation is necessary
in the case of blast furnaces, coke ovens and power stations, other
plants such as steel works and rolling mills can be shut down more
frequently. Nevertheless, the high cost of shutting down and
restarting such plant serves as an incentive to avoid daily shut-
downs, and to shut down only at weekly intervals. It is even
frequently found that steel works and rolling mills are operated
continuously for purely economic reasons, or to meet a need for

---

[1] M. Maurice: Le travail par équipes en France (Paris
University, Institut des sciences sociales du travail, 1962).
This study was conducted for the division of social affairs of
the European Economic Community.

increased output. Other departments then have to be operated continuously or semi-continuously in order to ensure the co-ordination
or continuity of the various stages of production; these may
include works transport, mechanical or electrical maintenance,
scrap yards or finishing shops.

It should be noted that this kind of chain reaction leading
to the spread of shift work can be more clearly seen in large plants
than in those of moderate size; in the case of the former, production organisation is called upon to achieve a higher degree of
integration.

The state of the market also plays an important part in the
organisation of shift work. If it is satisfactory, the plant will
be fully utilised; repairs and some of the maintenance required
will then be carried out on Sundays. In the opposite case, not only
will work be restricted to the working days of the week, but daily
shut-downs or pauses may sometimes be necessary.

In order to meet these various technical, organisational or
economic requirements, shift work in iron and steel works therefore
calls for a complex organisation making use of several rotation
systems, as already noted in Chapter III.

Chemicals

In the chemical industry, shift work is also used for
different reasons, both technical and economic in character.

The technical reasons are often the most important. In this
industry, continuous processes are dependent on the chemical reaction of the raw materials under the influence of physical agents
such as heat, pressure, or electricity; in contrast to engineering
operations, they cannot be shut down to bring them into step with
normal work schedules. Here again, however, technical requirements
sometimes coincide with economic advantage. This is the case when
it is necessary to operate costly installations continuously, by
means of an increase in the daily or weekly hours of work, or with
heated equipment where shut-down and start-up are particularly
difficult. In the latter case, which is common in this industry,
where materials that cannot be allowed to cool down are processed
at temperature, any premature shut-down deviating from the prescribed cycle of operations would markedly increase manufacturing
costs.

The tendency has been noted, in addition, in recent decades,
for shift work to become general in sectors where technical
requirements alone are not the determining factor. In those cases
shift work is most commonly a means of increasing output, of using
production capacity more fully, of reducing costs or of amortising
costly plant more rapidly. Undertakings then adopt shift work more
readily if they are continually faced with the need to increase
their investments. For heavy chemicals, in fact, investments
sometimes amount to as much as twice the annual turnover. Under
these conditions, such a rate of capitalisation, for equipment
that depreciates rapidly, serves as an incentive to the adoption
of this method of working.

It should be noted that the state of the market, or even a wide range of products, may lead to changes in the organisation of shift work over the year in a given factory. Thus the workers may have to change in succession from continuous to semi-continuous operation, and even to normal day work, at intervals of a few months, depending on production requirements.

The introduction of shift work may, in turn, have a positive effect on productivity in the chemical industry. For example a meeting of experts on productivity in manufacturing industries, held under ILO auspices, recommended that a larger number of shifts should be worked "where adequate markets exist, where supplies of materials and of labour are sufficient and where overhead costs represent a substantial proportion of total costs of production."[1]

Natural Textiles

In this sector of economic activity shift work has become increasingly widespread in the majority of countries over the last decade. It would seem that in some countries this development must continue, if the factors that have contributed to the adoption of this method of working in the industry are taken into account: these are essentially economic in character, linked with technological progress. Textile undertakings have to keep up with technological progress by the purchase of modern equipment, while amortising this equipment more rapidly, and they also have to reduce as much as possible investment in equipment that is continually becoming out of date. In addition to these two main factors, there is international competition, which is particularly keen in this sector of economic activity. It is more profitable, in fact, to buy a given number of modern looms and to operate them with successive shifts round the clock, in order to amortise them quickly and, after they have been written off, to buy more advanced equipment, than to buy two or three times as many looms at once and to operate them on a single shift, amortisation then being slower, so that there is a risk that the equipment will become out of date before it is written off.

Thus the increasingly rapid introduction of modern machines, of semi-automatic looms and more advanced methods of working, coupled with increasingly intense competition, has, in recent years, encouraged the adoption of shift work, and will certainly continue to do so in the future. It should be noted, however, that continuous operation is not necessary here; even when three-shift working is used, there is a break at the weekend, except in special cases. The introduction of a night shift in the textile industry, in addition, gives rise to serious social problems, because of the preponderance of female labour.

----

[1] "Practical methods of increasing productivity in manufacturing industries", _International Labour Review_, Vol. LXVII, No. 4, April 1953, p. 325.

Synthetic Textiles and
Similar Products

In this sector of economic activity, the reasons for the
adoption of shift work are fairly similar to those analysed in the
case of the industries previously considered, especially the
chemical industry and the natural fibres industry. The manufacture
of artificial and synthetic textiles can, in fact, be divided up
into two stages-

- the chemical stage, from the processing of the raw materials
  to spinning (including washing, bleaching and desulfurisation);

- the textile stage, including all the finishing operations
  (twisting, winding, sorting, etc.).

At the chemical stage, manufacture involves the processing of
the raw materials, which undergo either chemical change or a change
in their physical state as a result of operations carried out at
precisely determined temperatures, pressures and equilibrium conditions. Any variation in these factors results either in
differences in the quality of the textiles produced, or even, as a
result of the chemical or physical changes occurring in the plant,
to the shutting down of production. Because of the nature of the
manufacturing process, continuous operation, without a break at the
weekend, is an absolute technical necessity.

In the textile stage, two types of operation can be distinguished.
Certain operations, such as sorting, are usually carried out by means
of normal day work. In contrast, other operations, such as twisting
and winding, require the use of shift work for economic reasons:
the machines used for operations of this type are becoming increasingly complex and costly, and depreciate rapidly; it is therefore
necessary to utilise production capacity as fully as possible.
Even at the textile stage of manufacture, therefore, the trend is
towards continuous operation.

In addition, the weight of the unit of yarn is gradually
increasing in modern looms, with the aim, in particular, of reducing
the amount of handling of the yarn and the number of pieces. In
certain processes the weights to be handled are too great for this
to be done with ease by women, so that there is a tendency for
female labour, hitherto regarded as an obstacle to the general
adoption of three-shift working, to be eliminated. Already, in
certain regions, the work force is coming increasingly to consist
of men.

Thus, in this industry as well, the technical and economic
reasons for the adoption of shift work are closely linked.

Petroleum

This branch of industry, in which all operations from
extraction to marketing are integrated to a fairly high degree,
is of particular interest from the point of view of this study.
The adoption or organisation of shift work is justified, in this
case, for various technical and economic reasons, but also for
reasons linked with the problems of traffic in urban areas and the
ever increasing use of cars and aircraft.

At the prospecting stage, three-shift working is necessary in the boring of wells; this applies not only to the well-boring team but also to some of the maintenance workers and the field geologists responsible for the investigation and examination of the muds. Continuous operation is also necessary in the extraction of the crude petroleum; a protection team must be responsible for continuous control and supervision of the wells in production. In the same way, transport by pipeline calls for continuous operation in the pumping and metering stations and at the terminals.

In refineries, processing also makes shift work necessary for a small proportion of the maintenance workers (repair work) and for the monitoring laboratories. The general tendency is to make increasing use of continuously operated installations, which tends to increase the number of shifts; on the other hand, the progress of automation also leads to a decrease in the size of the crews. Some of the staff of research laboratories may also be required to do continuous shift work in order to carry out tests or to supervise pilot plants.

In recent years distribution has also contributed to the extension of shift work. Increased consumption, both by individuals and by communities, has made it necessary to stagger deliveries; these are increasingly being made by two successive shifts. As far as supplies at airports are concerned, the need for supplies at all times may make a succession of deliveries necessary. Nevertheless, in this latter case, the use of the hydrant system, or in other words of automatic supply points dispersed throughout the airport, is tending to reduce the importance of successive deliveries.

Finally, shift work has been adopted in the head offices of the oil companies, in the accounting and statistical departments where computers are used: in those departments work is organised in two shifts (sometimes with partial overlapping), or even in three.

Thus, at the different operational stages of this branch of industry, shift work is used for both technical and economic reasons, and is becoming one of the characteristic features of the industry.

Cement Works and Lime Kilns

In the manufacture of cement, the working rhythm of the worker is determined, in the case of a section of the work force, by the operation of the kilns which, for technical reasons, must not be shut down for any reason whatsoever. Workers and supervisory staff therefore work a continuous three-shift system. The grinding of the clinker is also a continuous process, so that it is possible to keep pace with the kilns without having to install an excessive number of grinders, which are extremely expensive.

In addition to those sections of the plant where continuous operation is technically necessary, however, it fairly frequently happens that, in a period of increasing demand, certain intermittent processes such as quarrying, crushing and distribution, go over to two-shift working; if these processes had to be operated with only a single shift, investment in equipment would be required, and the amortisation of this equipment would inevitably be reflected in costs.

Sugar Milling and Refining

The case of a branch of the food industry, having technological features differing considerably from those of the industries previously discussed, will now be considered.

The essential reason for the adoption of shift work in this industry (in sugar refineries) lies in the need to avoid shutting down certain processes or certain types of plant; this would lead either to the rapid deterioration of the raw materials or the materials being processed, or to blockages in the equipment or damage to it.

The seasonal nature of industry of this type also calls for a special form of work organisation at certain times of the year (harvesting and the associated operations occupy a period of 10 to 14 weeks). During this period, a system of two or three shifts is worked; night work by women may even be permitted.[1] Even outside this special period, however, the three-shift system is tending to become generally used for economic reasons (amortisation of modern equipment, which is sometimes automated). Certain undertakings then prefer gradually to replace by men the women workers traditionally employed in this industry. A semi-continuous three-shift system is then generally adopted, with a break at the weekend, except in the case of certain processes where a shut-down would lead to the deterioration of products in the course of processing or to blockages, which would be very costly to put right, in certain types of plant.

Automobile manufacture

Shift work is increasingly important in this industry, as in most branches of the engineering and electrical engineering industry. Whereas continuous or semi-continuous three-shift working is restricted to certain types of plant (foundries, power stations), one-third or two-thirds of the workers may sometimes be operating on a two-shift system. The reasons for the adoption of this method of working are essentially economic in character. In order to bring out a new model, a considerable amount of time has to be spent on design work and on the manufacture of the prototype. The investment in plant of different kinds, in turn, calls for a rapid rate of amortisation for a model whose commercial life may often be only a few years. This process is speeded up, in addition, by competition between the different companies, at both the national and international levels. The machines themselves have to be frequently replaced in order to keep pace with technical progress (it is estimated that 60 to 70 per cent of the machines are obsolete before they are worn out).

Under these conditions, shift work appears to provide an effective means of ensuring the rapid amortisation of the plant and equipment. The two-shift system is flexible enough to enable hours of work to be increased at rush periods, for example when a new model is being brought out or when there is an increase in demand as a result of the opening up of a new market.

---

[1] For example, under section 56 of Book II of the French Labour Code.

Electronic Data Processing

The use of computers is rapidly expanding, and the effects of this expansion on the use of shift work will be described here, both in the case of services forming an integral part of industrial or commercial establishments, and in that of undertakings whose main function is data processing. An ILO report, published as long ago as 1959, pointed out that "automation in offices" had "introduced shift work in types of employment where it had seldom been customary before".[1]

In contrast to the cases previously considered, where mainly manual workers are concerned (although, in most cases, shift work inevitably involves supervisors, managers, engineers or technicians, but only in limited numbers), data-processing services or establishments mainly employ non-manual workers, that is, salaried employees, technicians and engineers. Such workers are little used to shift work, and in the United Kingdom, for example, they have been called "the new shift workers".[2] Although the question of the acceptance or rejection of shift work will not be discussed here, it is important to determine the conditions under which it is carried out.[3] Because of the high cost of computers, electronic data processing installations keep their computers running for more than one standard shift per week.[4] Certain computers are capable of operating throughout the week (i.e. 168 hours), less about 16 hours for maintenance, but this is still exceptional. Some can operate for 80 hours a week, in two 40-hour shifts, an additional shift being available to deal with urgent work. A common characteristic of these services is their flexibility of operation; work schedules can be changed to keep pace with fluctuations in output. Whereas in certain undertakings night work is the exception, and is mainly used at the weekend, it is usual in others.[5]

---

[1] See ILO: Automation and non-manual workers, Labour and Automation Bulletin, No. 5 (Geneva, 1967), p. 17.

[2] See J. Larkcom: "The new shift workers", in Personnel Magazine (London), July 1965, and J. M. Towers: "Office staff, the new shift workers", in Production Engineering Research Association (PERA): The benefits and problems of shift working, A PERA symposium, 7th and 8th June 1966 (London).

[3] See Rhee, op. cit., pp. 135-137; L. Williams: "How automation affects the white-collar clerical employee", in Industrial Relations Counsellors: Computer technology: Concepts for management (New York, 1965), p. 28; W. H. Scott (ed.): Office automation (Paris, OECD, 1965); United States Bureau of Labor Statistics: "Impact of office automation in the insurance industry", Bulletin No. 1468 (Washington, 1966).

[4] See United States Civil Service Commission, Bureau of Programs and Standards: Personnel impact of automation in the federal service (Washington, 1957), p. 17.

[5] An inquiry conducted in 1965 by the Industrial Society (London) among 24 undertakings showed that five of them had data-processing services operating for 24 hours a day, five others worked for 16 hours a day and the remainder for between 12 and 16 hours (see Industrial Welfare Society: Shift work in offices, Information Survey and Report Series, No. 126 (London, 1965)).

Another characteristic of this type of work is the variation
in the length of the shifts; depending on the workload, it is
sometimes necessary for a shift to be extended for several hours.[1]

It should also be pointed out that some undertakings and
services have already reduced the weekly hours of work to less than
40; this was the case in 18 out of the 24 undertakings studied in
the above-mentioned inquiry conducted in the United Kindgom in 1965.
This reduction in the hours of work is no doubt one of the main
factors in making shift work more attractive to a labour force that
is often initially hostile to it. In contrast, the extension of
night work may have repercussions on the structure of the work
force hitherto employed, since the legislation in force in most
countries prohibits or restricts night work by women and young
people.[2]

Opinions seem to differ, however, as to the effect of automation on hours of work in offices. Thus the ILO publication on
automation and non-manual workers states that "extended hours of
work are common with automated office equipment, and that this trend
will become more marked"[3], while the inquiry previously mentioned,
conducted by The Industrial Society, reported a tendency for hours
of work to be decreased. This conflict is only apparent; it is
more a reflection of the diversity of the situations existing in
the various sectors of economic activity or the stage of development of automation in offices and services in different countries.

An increase in the hours of work when shift work is adopted
tends to bring non-manual and manual workers together, in the same
way as their work schedules tend to make their working conditions
more similar.

It should be pointed out, in addition, that while automation
has the effect, at least in the initial stages of its use, of
increasing the hours of work, in non-automated sectors, in contrast,
it may indirectly have the opposite effect. Thus, in banks
"extension of hours for computer staff has been accompanied ... by
a shortening of hours for non-computer staff".[4]

---

[1] See "Effects of mechanisation and automation in offices",
International Labour Review, Vol. LXXXI, No. 2, pp. 154-173, No. 3,
pp. 255-273, and No. 4, pp. 350-369.

[2] It is known that some employers would like to see greater
flexibility in the legislation in this field.

[3] Automation and non-manual workers, op. cit., p. 17; other
ILO publications confirm the existence of a tendency for the hours
of work to be increased. See Manpower adjustment programmes:
I. France, Federal Republic of Germany, United Kingdom; II. Sweden,
USSR, United States, Labour and Automation Bulletins Nos. 4 and 6
(Geneva, 1967).

[4] Automation and non-manual workers, op. cit., p. 18.

Finally, recent studies have shown that the reduction in the labour force due to automation may vary widely; economies in staff sometimes amounted to as much as one-third of the total, but could be very small or non-existent in other cases. The introduction of shift work sometimes results initially in an increase in staff. This whole range of problems is often the subject of negotiations between trade unions and employers.[1]

Thus, both in industry and in offices and services, shift work is becoming increasingly common, for economic rather than for technical reasons, although in most cases these two types of factor are inter-related; the examples of automation and electronic data processing provide a perfect illustration of this. Nevertheless, the spread of shift work does not necessarily mean, in the longer term, that the number of workers affected, whether manual or non-manual, will also increase.[2]

---

[1] Automation and non-manual workers, op. cit., pp. 50-57 and 103-105.

[2] United Kingdom, Ministry of Labour: Computers in offices, Manpower Studies, No. 4 (London, HM Stationery Office, 1965), particularly pp. 17-24 and p. 34, and Appendix 15, p. 52, idem, Introduction of shift working, op. cit., pp. 8-9; ILO: Automation and non-manual workers, op. cit.

2. Statutory Restrictions on Night Work
    and Sunday Work Affecting Shift Work
    in the Major Industrialised Countries

Legislation on shift work has been gradually evolved as general
labour legislation has developed, mainly in the industrialised
countries[1]; nevertheless, there are differences between one country
and another. It is not intended here to present an exhaustive
analysis of the legislation; a brief account will be given of the
trends in each country with regard to the following two particular
aspects of shift work with which labour legislation is concerned[2]:

- night work, which is directly related to the working conditions
   of children, young people and women, protective measures having
   been taken with regard to these two categories of workers;

- Sunday work; this concerns all categories of workers.

Night Work

It should be pointed out here that the Night Work (Women)
Convention (Revised), 1948 (No. 89) and the Night Work of Young
Persons (Industry) Convention (Revised), 1948 (No. 90) prohibit
night work by women and young people; the term "night", in the
case of women, is defined to mean a period of at least 11
consecutive hours, including an interval of at least seven consecutive hours falling between 10 p.m. and 7 a.m. and, in the case
of young people, a period of at least 12 consecutive hours, which
also includes an interval of seven consecutive hours falling between
10 p.m. and 7 a.m.

In general, night work by young people and women is prohibited
in the countries of the European Communities, although provision is
made for exemptions in certain circumstances; there must be a
gap of 11 or 12 hours between the periods of work in any given day.

The special provisions enacted in the different countries are
given below.

---

[1] As far as is known to the author, only two major industrialised countries have rewritten their labour legislation, and have
revised it in a fairly radical manner, namely Italy, in 1934, and
Belgium, in 1964. See: European Economic Community: Le travail
dominical dans les Etats membres de la CEE, op. cit., Chapter I.
The text of the relevant Italian laws is given in ILO: Legislative
series, 1934, It. 3 and 6, and that of the Belgian laws in ibid.,
1964, Bel. 1 and 2.

[2] The use of shift work also involves other matters dealt with
in the labour legislation, including daily and weekly hours of work,
which have already been dealt with in the first part of Chapter VII.
References to studies dealing with particular aspects of the
legislation are given in the selected bibliography.

Federal Republic of Germany: No work of any kind may be
performed by young people or women between 8 p.m. and 6 a.m.[1];
the definition of night work in the majority of collective agreements includes the same period of time. Provision is, however,
made for exemptions in certain branches of industry, particularly
in the transport and hotel industries, where the limit is extended
to 11 p.m.

Belgium: Belgium is one of the few countries in which night
work is prohibited for all categories of workers between 8 p.m.
and 6 a.m.; numerous exemptions exist, however, for male workers
in the industries and services in which continuous operation is
necessary. In the case of women and children, a period of rest
of 11 consecutive hours, including the period from 10 p.m. to
5 a.m., is compulsory between two periods of work. A royal order
of 24 October 1967[2], which came into force on 1 January 1968,
permits the initial and final times mentioned above to be changed
from 11 p.m. to 12 midnight and from 5 a.m. to 6 a.m. respectively
when shift work is carried out in an undertaking where a five-day
week is worked and where each shift works more than 8 hours a day.

France: Night work, between 10 p.m. and 5 a.m., by women
and by young people under 18 years of age is prohibited[3]; provision is made for exemptions, in particular for limited periods
in seasonal industries and in certain services, such as the postal
services and telecommunications, hospitals, and air and maritime
transport.

Italy: Night work by women is prohibited, whatever their
age; the same applies to young people under 16 years of age.[4]
The period of rest must comprise 11 consecutive hours, including
the period between 10 p.m. and 5 a.m.

Netherlands: Night work, between 6 p.m. and 7 a.m., is
prohibited except in the case of shift work, for which exemptions
have been provided. For women, a period of rest of at least
12 consecutive hours is prescribed, including the period between
10 p.m. and 6 a.m., and no exemptions are permitted; the same
applies to young people less than 18 years of age.

United Kingdom: In principle, night work by women and by
young people under 18 years of age is prohibited between 10 p.m.
and 6 a.m.; provision has been made for exemptions in certain
industries, and in particular in those industries in which operation is continuous, where young people over 16 years of age may
do night work under certain conditions.[5]

---

[1] Protection of Young Persons Act, dated 30 April 1938. See
ILO: Legislative series, 1938, Ger. 5.

[2] See ILO: Legislative series, 1967, Bel. 3.

[3] Night Work (Women and Children) Act, dated 24 January 1925.
Ibid., 1925, Fr. 1.

[4] See ILO: Legislative series, 1934, It. 6, and 1967, It. 1.

[5] Additional information on this subject is given in United
Kingdom, Department of Employment and Productivity: Hours of
employment of women and young persons employed in factories, A
report (London, HM Stationery Office, 1969).

In other countries - the Scandinavian countries, Australia, Canada, the United States - provisions applicable to night work also exist; in the three latter countries, however, it is difficult to give an over-all picture of the legislation because of the federal system of government under which the statutory requirement may vary from one constituent state or province to another.

Night work by young people under 16 or 18 years of age is prohibited in the Scandinavian countries (Denmark, Norway and Sweden). In Norway and Sweden night work by all workers is prohibited, except under certain conditions such as continuous operation, whereas in Denmark no restrictions on night work are imposed in the case of adult workers.

In the United States no federal law applicable to night work exists; in many states, however, it is prohibited for women or young people or both.

In Australia, most states prohibit night work by young people, but only in New South Wales is night work by women prohibited.

It should be pointed out, finally, that in most countries in which night work by women is prohibited the view is being expressed, generally by the employers, that the legislation in this field should be made more flexible; in most cases this view is opposed by the trade unions.

Sunday Work

As already pointed out, the extension of continuous shift work has had the effect of dividing the work up between different shifts, not only over the 24 hours of the day, but also over the seven days of the week, including nights and Sundays. In the latter case, it has thus become increasingly difficult to reconcile the requirements of continuous operation in certain industries or services with the social, family or religious requirement that Sunday should be the weekly day of rest.

It will be remembered, in this connection, that two opposing points of view exist: of these, one stresses the weekly nature of the rest period, thus reflecting a desire to preserve the health of the worker and to enable him to participate in family and social life; the other gives priority to Sunday as the day of rest, for religious reasons and in order to preserve family life. The legislation of certain countries (in particular, France and Italy) seems to have been based on the first point of view, while the second appears to have influenced the legislation of the Federal Republic of Germany and of the Netherlands.

Although the International Labour Organisation "has not yet directly approached the problem of Sunday work"[1], this question has often been mentioned or dealt with in connection with that of weekly rest, with which two Conventions[2], in particular, have been concerned.

---

[1] European Economic Community: Le travail dominical dans les Etats membres de la CEE, op. cit., Chapter I, p. 8.

[2] The Weekly Rest (Industry) Convention, 1921 (No. 14) and the Weekly Rest (Commerce and Offices) Convention, 1957 (No. 106).

Belgium: The question of Sunday rest is governed in Belgium by a law of 6 July 1943. Workers may be regularly employed on Sunday, but only by way of exemption, particularly in the special case of continuous operation. A compensatory period of rest must be given in the six days following the Sunday concerned, varying in length from a half to a whole day, if more than four hours are worked on Sunday. When night work is continued until 6 a.m. on Sunday, the workers concerned may not go back to work until 6 a.m. on Monday. No exemptions may be made in the case of boys under 16 or girls or women under 21. In industries where operation is continuous, however, the Crown may authorise the employment of girls and women between 16 and 21 years of age over the seven days of the week under certain conditions.

France: The same worker may not be employed for more than six days in any one week, and a weekly period of rest of 24 consecutive hours on Sunday is compulsory. Provision is made for exemptions in the case of continuous operation (section 39 of Book II of the Labour Code), and for a period of rest of 24 consecutive hours in the case of Sunday work, provided that the number of periods of rest of 24 consecutive hours are always equal at least to the number of weeks in the period under consideration. Exemptions generally apply to male workers over 18 years of age, but neither to younger people nor to women. It should be pointed out that the provision of the weekly period of rest in factories under continuous operation was facilitated by the extension of the 40-hour week in 1936; the organisation of a four-crew system gives a weekly average of 42 hours over a period of 12 weeks, while a period of rest of 24 hours per week must be provided in any case.

Federal Republic of Germany: The protection of Sunday as the day of rest dates back to the provisions of a law of 21 June 1869. Article 139 of the Constitution of the Federal Republic of Germany states that: "Sunday and public holidays recognised by the State shall be protected by the law as days of rest and spiritual elevation". It is just this latter concept of Sunday as a day of rest that has given rise to difficulties in the recent extension of shift work and of the "rotating week".[1]

The Young Persons (Protection of Employment) Act, 1960[2], lays down that young people may not be employed on Sundays and public holidays; provision is made for exemptions only in the hotel industry, places of entertainment, agriculture and inland navigation. An order made in 1943 provides that women who have children under 14 years of age and for whom adequate help is not available may be exempted on request from work authorised, as an exception, on Sundays and public holidays. Provision is also made for exemptions in certain branches of industry for persons over 18 years of age; in that case, the worker is entitled to a period of rest of 36 consecutive hours and to one Sunday out of three.

---

[1] See Otto Neuloh, Rudolf Braun and Erich Werner: Die durchlaufende Arbeitsweise (Tübingen, J.C.B. Mohr, 1961), in particular pp. 57, 152 and 155.

[2] See ILO: Legislative series, 1960, Ger. F.R. 2.

In the iron and steel industry, as also in the paper industry, earlier regulations of the Federal Council have been superseded by new provisions (ordinances of 7 July 1961 and 5 November 1963). These new regulations provide, in principle, for 26 Sundays off per year; the length of the rest period is 40 hours and must include the whole of Sunday, round the clock. If a Sunday is worked, a compensatory period of rest of at least 24 hours is to be granted in the same or the preceding week.

Italy: Under the provisions of a law of 22 February 1934[1], the length of the weekly period of rest must be 24 hours, from midnight on Saturday to midnight on Sunday; the corresponding exemptions refer neither to sex nor to age. In the case of shift work, the period of rest on Sunday begins at the time at which each shift is relieved.

An unbroken period of rest of at least 24 hours must, however, be given to women, whatever their age, and to young people under 14 years of age (section 4 of the law mentioned above).

Netherlands: Laws of 1919 and 1953 recognise the principle of Sunday as the day of rest. Provision is made, however, in an order of 1936[2], for exemptions from this principle for certain types of work (maintenance, repair and shift work).

In the case of continuous operation, Sunday work is authorised for men, provided that they are given a period of rest of 32 consecutive hours, of which 20 hours must be on a Sunday at least once every three weeks, or of 36 consecutive hours including a Sunday at least once every four weeks.

Sunday work is absolutely prohibited for women and young people under 18 years of age. For women over 18 exemptions are possible in non-industrial activities such as work in the retail trade, in offices, or in hotels. In industry, provision is made for very limited exemptions, in particular in the food industry and in seasonal industries.

Additional information on Sunday work is available in the previously mentioned publication[3] of the European Economic Community.

---

[1] ILO: Legislative series, 1934, It. 3.

[2] Ibid., 1936, Neth. 2.

[3] Le travail dominical dans les Etats membres de la CEE, op. cit.

3. Systems of Organisation of Shift Work

A. Further examples of shift
   work systems[1]

An account will first be given of systems having special features, as compared with those most commonly used, mentioned in Chapter III.

(a) Continuous four-crew working
    with rotation every two days
    (Average working week: 42 hours)

The length of the complete cycle is 8 weeks; it takes 8 days for one crew (A, B, C or D) to come back to the same shift, and 8 weeks to come back to the same shift on the same day of the week.

The order of the shifts and the frequency of changeover are as follows: two morning shifts, two afternoon shifts, two night shifts and two rest days.

This routine gives two free Sundays every 8 weeks, and these Sundays are accompanied, in turn, by a Saturday and a Monday.

Day of the week	Rest	4 a.m.-12 noon	12 noon-8 p.m.	8 p.m.-4 a.m.	Rest	4 a.m.-12 noon	12 noon-8 p.m.	8 p.m.-4 a.m.
Monday	C	A	B	D	B	D	C	A
Tuesday	C	A	B	D	B	D	C	A
Wednesday	D	C	A	B	A	B	D	C
Thursday	D	C	A	B	A	B	D	C
Friday	B	D	C	A	C	A	B	D
Saturday	B	D	C	A	C	A	B	D
Sunday	A	B	D	C	D	C	A	B
Monday	A	B	D	C	D	C	A	B
Tuesday	C	A	B	D	B	D	C	A
Wednesday	C	A	B	D	B	D	C	A
Thursday	D	C	A	B	A	B	D	C
Friday	D	C	A	B	A	B	D	C
Saturday	B	D	C	A	C	A	B	D
Sunday	B	D	C	A	C	A	B	D
Monday	A	B	D	C	D	C	A	B
Tuesday	A	B	D	C	D	C	A	B
Wednesday	C	A	B	D	B	D	C	A
Thursday	C	A	B	D	B	D	C	A
Friday	D	C	A	B	A	B	D	C
Saturday	D	C	A	B	A	B	D	C
Sunday	B	D	C	A	C	A	B	D
Monday	B	D	C	A	C	A	B	D
Tuesday	A	B	D	C	D	C	A	B
Wednesday	A	B	D	C	D	C	A	B
Thursday	C	A	B	D	B	D	C	A
Friday	C	A	B	D	B	D	C	A
Saturday	D	C	A	B	A	B	D	C
Sunday	D	C	A	B	A	B	D	C

[1] Information is given in Industrial Welfare Society: Shift work, current practices in Great Britain, op. cit., on systems of shift rotation; in particular, detailed information is given from which other systems can be constructed to take account of certain requirements. See, in particular, pp. 21 and 31.

(b) <u>Continuous four-crew working</u>
<u>with rotation every three days</u>
<u>and then every two days</u>
(Average working week: 42 hours)

The length of the complete cycle is 28 days; it gives one free Sunday every four weeks. Shifts are rotated after two days, again after another two days, and then after three days. Three days of rest (72 hours) complete the cycle.

Day of the week	Rest	4 a.m.-12 noon	12 noon-8 p.m.	8 p.m.-4 a.m.
Monday	B	A	D	C
Tuesday	B	A	D	C
Wednesday	C	B	A	D
Thursday	C	B	A	D
Friday	D	C	B	A
Saturday	D	C	B	A
Sunday	D	C	B	A
Monday	A	D	C	B
Tuesday	A	D	C	B
Wednesday	B	A	D	C
Thursday	B	A	D	C
Friday	C	B	A	D
Saturday	C	B	A	D
Sunday	C	B	A	D
Monday	D	C	B	A
Tuesday	D	C	B	A
Wednesday	A	D	C	B
Thursday	A	D	C	B
Friday	B	A	D	C
Saturday	B	A	D	C
Sunday	B	A	D	C
Monday	C	B	A	D
Tuesday	C	B	A	D
Wednesday	D	C	B	A
Thursday	D	C	B	A
Friday	A	D	C	B
Saturday	A	D	C	B
Sunday	A	D	C	B

(c) <u>Continuous four-crew working</u>
<u>with rotation every four days</u>
(Average working week: 47 hours)

The length of the complete cycle is 16 weeks; it gives four free Sundays per cycle, the last being preceded by a free Saturday.

The order of the shifts is as follows: four morning shifts, one rest day, four afternoon shifts, one rest day, four night shifts, two rest days.

Day of the week	Rest	4.30a.m.-12.30p.m.	12.30p.m.-8.30p.m.	8.30p.m.-4.30a.m.	Rest	4.30a.m.-12.30p.m.	12.30p.m.-8.30p.m.	8.30p.m.-4.30a.m.
Monday	D	A	C	B	B	A	D	C
Tuesday	C	A	D	B	A	B	D	C
Wednesday	B	A	D	C	D	B	A	C
Thursday	B	A	D	C	C	B	A	D
Friday	A	B	D	C	C	B	A	D
Saturday	D	B	A	C	B	C	A	D
Sunday	C	B	A	D	A	C	B	D
Monday	C	B	A	D	D	C	B	A
Tuesday	B	C	A	D	D	C	B	A
Wednesday	A	C	B	D	C	D	B	A
Thursday	D	C	B	A	B	D	C	A
Friday	D	C	B	A	A	D	C	B
Saturday	C	D	B	A	A	D	C	B
Sunday	B	D	C	A	D	A	C	B
Monday	A	D	C	B	C	A	D	B
Tuesday	A	D	C	B	B	A	D	C
Wednesday	D	A	C	B	B	A	D	C
Thursday	C	A	D	B	A	B	D	C
Friday	B	A	D	C	D	B	A	C
Saturday	B	A	D	C	C	B	A	D
Sunday	A	B	D	C	C	B	A	D
Monday	D	B	A	C	B	C	A	D
Tuesday	C	B	A	D	A	C	B	D
Wednesday	C	B	A	D	D	C	B	A
Thursday	B	C	A	D	D	C	B	A
Friday	A	C	B	D	C	D	B	A
Saturday	D	C	B	A	B	D	C	A
Sunday	D	C	B	A	A	D	C	B
Monday	C	D	B	A	A	D	C	B
Tuesday	B	D	C	A	D	A	C	B
Wednesday	A	D	C	B	C	A	D	B
Thursday	A	D	C	B	B	A	D	C
Friday	D	A	C	B	B	A	D	C
Saturday	C	A	D	B	A	B	D	C
Sunday	B	A	D	C	D	B	A	C

(d) Continuous working with seven half-crews (weekly rotation)
(Average working week: 46 1/8 hours)

This system is used in the French iron and steel industry, which employs a large number of workers. Each shift is worked by two half-crews; six half-crews work while the seventh rests, hence the name "the seven half-crew system".

The length of the cycle is seven weeks, divided up into 42 working days and seven rest days. Shifts are rotated every seven days and are separated by a rest period of 48 hours, except for the changeover from the night shift to the morning shift, where the rest period is only 24 hours; this system gives one Saturday and Sunday in succession every seven weeks. The total number of hours of rest is 264.

The seven half-crews are designated by the letters A, B, C, D, E, F and G. The easiest way of understanding the table for this system is to follow one particular half-crew over the entire cycle, say, half-crew A, for example, which begins the cycle.

Day of the week	6 a.m.-2 p.m.		2 p.m.-10 p.m.		10 p.m.-6 a.m.		Rest	
Monday	A	D	E	F	B	G	C	
Tuesday	A	D	C	F	B	G	E	
Wednesday	A	D	C	F	E	G	B	
Thursday	A	B	C	F	E	G	D	
Friday	A	B	C	D	E	G	F	
Saturday	A	B	C	D	E	F	G	
Sunday	A	B	C	D	E	F	G	
Monday	G	B	C	D	E	F	A	48 hrs
Tuesday	G	B	A	D	E	F	C	
Wednesday	G	B	A	D	C	F	E	
Thursday	G	E	A	D	C	F	B	
Friday	G	E	A	B	C	F	D	
Saturday	G	E	A	B	C	D	F	
Sunday	G	E	A	B	C	D	F	
Monday	F	E	A	B	C	D	G	
Tuesday	F	E	G	B	C	D	A	48 hrs
Wednesday	F	E	G	B	A	D	C	
Thursday	F	C	G	B	A	D	E	
Friday	F	C	G	E	A	D	B	
Saturday	F	C	G	E	A	B	D	
Sunday	F	C	G	E	A	B	D	
Monday	D	C	G	E	A	B	F	
Tuesday	D	C	F	E	A	B	G	
Wednesday	D	C	F	E	G	B	A	24 hrs
Thursday	D	A	F	E	G	B	C	
Friday	D	A	F	C	G	B	E	
Saturday	D	A	F	C	G	E	B	
Sunday	D	A	F	C	G	E	B	
Monday	B	A	F	C	G	E	D	
Tuesday	B	A	D	C	G	E	F	
Wednesday	B	A	D	C	F	E	G	
Thursday	B	G	D	C	F	E	A	48 hrs
Friday	B	G	D	A	F	E	C	
Saturday	B	G	D	A	F	C	E	
Sunday	B	G	D	A	F	C	E	
Monday	E	G	D	A	F	C	B	
Tuesday	E	G	B	A	F	C	D	
Wednesday	E	G	B	A	D	C	F	
Thursday	E	F	B	A	D	C	G	
Friday	E	F	B	G	D	C	A	48 hrs
Saturday	E	F	B	G	D	A	C	
Sunday	E	F	B	G	D	A	C	
Monday	C	F	B	G	D	A	E	
Tuesday	C	F	E	G	D	A	B	
Wednesday	C	F	E	G	B	A	D	
Thursday	C	D	E	G	B	A	F	
Friday	C	D	E	F	B	A	G	
Saturday	C	D	E	F	B	G	A	
Sunday	C	D	E	F	B	G	A	48 hrs

(e) <u>Continuous four-crew working</u>
   (Average working week: 40 hours)

   This system, which has the advantage of giving a 40-hour
week for each crew, has a cycle of 21 weeks. The cycle given in
the table is for worker No. 1 starting from week No. 1.

Order of weeks	Days of the week							Number of shifts worked
	M	T	W	T	F	S	S	
1	-	M	M	A	A	N	N	6
2	-	-	-	M	M	A	A	4
3	N	N	-	-	-	M	M	4
4	A	A	N	N	-	-	-	4
5	M	M	A	A	N	N	-	6
6	-	-	M	M	A	A	N	5
7	N	-	-	-	M	M	A	4
8	A	N	N	-	-	-	M	4
9	M	A	A	N	N	-	-	5
10	-	M	M	A	A	N	N	6
11	N	-	-	M	M	A	A	5
12	A	N	N	-	-	M	M	5
13	M	A	A	N	N	-	-	5
14	-	M	M	A	A	N	N	6
15	N	-	-	M	M	A	A	5
16	A	N	N	-	-	M	M	5
17	M	A	A	N	N	-	-	5
18	-	M	M	A	A	N	N	6
19	N	-	-	M	M	A	A	5
20	A	N	N	-	-	M	M	5
21	M	A	A	N	N	-	-	5
							Total:	105
							Average:	5

Notes: M = morning shift (6 a.m.-2 p.m.)
        A = afternoon shift (2 p.m.-10 p.m.)
        N = night shift (10 p.m.-6 a.m.)

B. <u>Case studies on the adoption of
    new shift rotation systems</u>

   Of the following two case studies, the first relates to an
experiment on changing the frequency of rotation - from a long
cycle of rotation to a short cycle - in the United Kingdom, and
the second gives an account of Soviet experience, taking into
account both the economic policy and the social policy peculiar
to the USSR.

(a) <u>Change of frequency of shift</u>
    <u>rotation</u>

Change from a long cycle to a short cycle[1]

In a chemical undertaking in the United Kingdom, a rapidly
rotating system was introduced at the request of the workers, of
whom two-thirds voted in favour of the new system. The system
previously in use had been based on a weekly rotation (seven days),
as shown in the table (this shows the cycle for a worker over the
four-week period). The average working week is 42 hours in both
cases.

Day of the week	Old system			
	1st week	2nd week	3rd week	4th week
Monday	6am-2pm	free	10pm-6am	2pm-10pm
Tuesday	6am-2pm	free	10pm-6am	2pm-10pm
Wednesday	6am-2pm	10pm-6am	free	2pm-10pm
Thursday	6am-2pm	10pm-6am	free	2pm-10pm
Friday	6am-2pm	10pm-6am	2pm-10pm	free
Saturday	6am-12.30pm	10pm-6am	12.30pm-10pm	free
Sunday	free	10pm-6am	2pm-10pm	2pm-10pm
	New system			
Monday	6am-2pm	free	10pm-6am	2pm-10pm
Tuesday	6am-2pm	free	10pm-6am	2pm-10pm
Wednesday	2pm-10pm	6am-2pm	free	10pm-6am
Thursday	2pm-10pm	6am-2pm	free	10pm-6am
Friday	10pm-6am	2pm-10pm	6am-2pm	free
Saturday	10pm-6am	12.30pm-10pm	6am-12.30pm	free
Sunday	free	10pm-6am	2pm-10pm	6am-2pm

In an undertaking in another industry (iron and steel) a system
which is similar to that just described but involves a shift
rotation regularly every two days was also adopted at the request
of the workers instead of the previous semi-continuous system with
a weekly rotation. The change, in this case, was associated with
a reduction in the average working week from 45 to 42 hours and
an increase in earnings by about 20 per cent. These factors
obviously facilitated the acceptance of the new system by the workers.

An inquiry conducted three years after these changes had been
made showed that in both cases the majority of the workers preferred
the new system. The reasons given were the following: better
conditions for rest and sleep, less interference with social life,
greater satisfaction on the part of the spouse, and less monotonous
work.

---

[1] J. Walker: "Frequent alternation of shifts on continuous
work", in <u>Occupational Psychology</u> (London, National Institute of
Industrial Psychology), Vol. 40, 1966, pp. 215-255.

The results of the inquiry showed that the workers preferred
to break the monotony of the work done during the week. They found
that the new system gave them greater opportunities to organise
their family and social life. They felt less tired; the most
objectionable shifts, such as the night shift, were worked for a
shorter period, and recovery from fatigue seemed thereby to be
made easier.

Although receptive to suggestions from the workers, the
employers had at first been hesitant. However, they admitted that
the management and communication difficulties that they had feared
have been overcome.

These cases, of course, are not necessarily held up as
examples to be followed, but they do show the advantage to be gained
by consulting the workers with regard to the organisation of the
method of working. They also show the advantage of systems that
are as flexible as possible, and that meet the individuals'
physiological, family and social needs.

(b) The experience of the USSR:
      the Ivanovo schedule[1]

The average working week in the USSR was shortened from
47.8 hours in 1956 to 40 in 1960.[2] Starting in 1962, the five-
day week was introduced on an experimental basis in many enterprises and, in 1967, the Presidium of the Supreme Soviet fixed the
length of the working week for non-agricultural workers at five
days, by doing away with the six-hour day worked on Saturday. Thus
the 41-hour working week provided for by Soviet legislation is
retained by increasing the daily hours of work from seven hours to
8 hours and 12 minutes from Monday to Friday.

It should be pointed out, in addition, that the recent reforms
in conditions of work in Soviet enterprises are also aimed at
eliminating night work, i.e., the third shift, wherever this is
technically possible.

While the introduction of the five-day week in enterprises
working one or two shifts does not give rise to any difficulties,
this is not true of enterprises where three shifts are worked.
Of the experiments carried out in this field, two types of
schedule adapted to the requirements of shift work deserve
attention.

The first, known as the "Ivanovo schedule", was introduced on
an experimental basis in 1963 in the textile factories of the
Ivanovo region. The operation of this schedule is illustrated
in the table shown below:

---

[1] See Kabaj: "Shift work and employment expansion: towards
an optimum pattern", op. cit., pp. 262-265.

[2] Under Soviet legislation the working week is 41 hours in
normal working conditions and 36 hours when the conditions are
particularly difficult.

Assignment	M	T	W	T	F	S	S	M	T	W	T	F	S	S	M	
Morning shift	A	A	A	A	A	B	B	B	B	B	C	C	C	C	C	
Afternoon shift	B	B	B	C	C	C	C	C	A	A	A	A	A	B	B	
Night shift	C					A					B					
Days off		C	C	B	B		A	A	C	C		B	B	A	A	etc.

Source: Ekonomicheskaya Gazeta (Moscow), No. 11, 1967, cited in
         Kabaj: "Shift work and employment expansion: Towards
         an optimum pattern", op. cit., pp. 263-264.

While, before the introduction of this schedule, the workers
worked seven hours a day for a six-day week, and were divided into
three crews who worked, in turn, a night shift of 8 to 9 hours
(there were then an average of 7 to 10 night shifts per month),
with the new schedule, the workers, while still being divided
into three crews, work two shifts for most of the time, namely,
one in the morning and one in the afternoon. The machines, however,
are operated seven days a week, each crew working for five
successive days on a particular shift and then having two days off.
The number of night shifts is reduced, since each worker now works
only one or two in each month.

This method of working, which has been adopted in other enterprises after a trial period, has two special advantages: it considerably reduces the amount of night work and allows workers two
days off per week. The loss of production that might result is
compensated for by the increase in the length of each shift and by
the adoption of continuous working with the elimination of the
weekly shut-down. This however, is precisely the main disadvantage
of the schedule: the two free days may be on any days of the week,
and do not necessarily fall on Saturdays and Sundays. From the
sociological inquiries conducted in this connection in the USSR,
certain categories of workers object to this system and would prefer
to continue to do night work so as to have two rest days at the
weekend.

In order to avoid this disadvantage, other schedules have
been developed, one of which is illustrated in the following table:

Example of rotating shift schedule
allowing regular days off

Assignment	M	T	W	T	F	S	S	M	T	W	T	F	S	S	M	
First and second week:																
Morning shift	A	A	A	A	A	A		B	B	B	B	B	B			
Afternoon shift	B	B	B	B	B			C	C	C	C	C				
Night shift	C	C	C	C	C			A	A	A	A	A				
Days off						B C	A B C						A C	A B C		
Third and fourth week:																
Morning shift	C	C	C	C	C	C		A	A	A	A	A	A		B	
Afternoon shift	A	A	A	A	A			B	B	B	B	B			C	
Night shift	B	B	B	B	B			C	C	C	C	C			A	
Days off						A B	A B C						B C	A B C		etc.

Source: See previous table.

In this "mixed" schedule, the morning and afternoon shifts work 8 hours and the night shift 7 hours. The workers on the morning shift have one day off per week, those on the afternoon and night shifts have two. Average weekly hours thus amount to 41 over the three-week cycle. Workers have more regular rest periods, but night shifts are not eliminated.

These examples are of interest mainly in showing the directions in which new solutions to the problems of shift work may be sought.

C. Shift work systems used in
    offices and in data
    processing

While a fairly wide variety of shift work systems are used in industry, they are often the result, as already pointed out, of local or industrial traditions. This is clearly not the case in more modern branches of economic activity which, for this reason, have often developed special shift work patterns. This is particularly true in the mechanical and electronic data processing. Since the reasons for the extension of shift work to this branch of economic activity have been given in Appendix 1, only information on the systems themselves will be given here.

As has already been emphasised, the main characteristic of the organisation of hours of work in this type of activity is flexibility. Nevertheless the organisation of work is gradually becoming more systematic as these establishments become increasingly specialised and their output increases. A two-shift or three-shift system may be used, or a combination of such systems.

With a two-shift system the shifts may be consecutive, as in industry: for example, one shift may work from 7 a.m. to 3 p.m. followed by another from 3 to 11 p.m. Other systems are also used, however, either with overlapping shifts (9 a.m. to 5 p.m. and 1 to 8.30 p.m.) or with shifts following on after a gap of a few hours (8.30 a.m. to 4.45 p.m., then 10 p.m. to 5.30 a.m.). This last system is widely used in the United Kingdom under the name of the day and night system.

When three shifts are used, working is generally semi-continuous; Sunday working is still the exception, and a five-day working week, from Monday to Friday, is common, Saturday morning being worked in case of emergency or used for maintenance.

It should be noted, however, that starting times are usually different from those in industry. While, in the latter, the commonest routines are 6 a.m. - 2 p.m., 2 - 10 p.m. and 10 p.m. - 6 a.m., or 4 a.m. - 12 noon, 12 noon - 8 p.m. and 8 p.m. - 4 a.m., widely varying routines are found where computers are used (for example, 9 a.m. - 3.30 p.m., 3.30 - 10.30 p.m. and 10.30 p.m. - 9 a.m.). It will be noted that the length of the day shift is six hours and a half or seven hours, while that of the night shift is ten hours and a half, but the rest period during the night shift is longer than that during the day shifts (three-quarters of an hour to an hour). Shift changeover may be every week or every fortnight, the latter arrangement being fairly common, especially

in the United Kingdom.   In contrast to the systems most commonly
used in industry, shifts may therefore be of unequal length.   The
tendency to reduce the length of the working week (which is often
less than 40 hours) in this branch of economic activity has already
been mentioned.[1]

The night work is generally done by men;   there may be two
crews made up of women on day work, together with three crews made
up of men.

---

[1] The choice of arrangement of work schedules seems to have
been influenced by the type of personnel involved, as if there
were one arrangement suitable for workers paid by the hour and
another for employees paid monthly.   Some interesting information,
in this connection, is given by Grossin in Le travail et le temps,
op. cit.

4. Statistics

As already pointed out in Chapter I, only a few countries have published statistics in this field. Statistical tables published by the Ministry of Labour in certain countries (France, Italy, Japan and the United Kingdom) are, however, reproduced below.

France

In France up to the present the Ministry of Labour has conducted three surveys with the aim of measuring the amount of shift work done in industrial and commercial establishments employing more than ten workers, with the exception of public services.[1]

1. Establishments where work was done in shifts and number of workers on shift work in the main branches of industry, 1963 (percentages)

Sector of economic activity	Establishments	Workers
All sectors	10.9	18.7
Industry	14.3	21.4
including:		
Petroleum and liquid fuels	26.1	47.5
Manufacture of metals	68.5	64.0
Textiles	42.9	44.7
Paper and board	38.6	36.8
Chemicals and rubber	27.7	35.4
Glass, ceramics and building materials	25.4	25.5
Printing	13.0	24.5
General engineering	9.4	13.5
Machine building	8.3	20.4
Electrical engineering	10.0	11.2
Agriculture and food	18.1	15.0

[1] These surveys were conducted in 1957, 1959 and 1963. The results issued by the statistical branch of the Ministry of Labour were published in Travail et main-d'oeuvre in 1957, and in the Revue française du travail in 1962 and 1965.

2. Increase in shift work in industrial
   establishments from 1957 to 1963
   (percentage of establishments in which
   shift work is done)

Industry	1957	1959	1963
Fabrication of metals	43.1	60.4	68.5
Textile industry	38.8	39.1	42.9
Paper and board	29.0	35.1	38.6
Chemicals and rubber	17.3	26.1	27.7
Glass and ceramics	15.2	22.0	25.4
Machine building	4.3	5.6	8.3
Printing	6.3	11.0	13.0

Italy

In the absence of government statistics, some of the results
of a survey conducted by the General Confederation of Italian
Industry and published in 1969[1] are given below.

1. Extent of shift work in certain branches of industry

Branches of industry	Establishments in which shift work is done (as a per cent of total establishments in the branch concerned)	Workers employed in establishments where shift work is done (as a per cent of all workers in the branch concerned)	Shift workers, as a per cent of the workers employed in the establishments where shift work is done
Metallurgy	100.0	100.0	82.9
Engineering	95.0	99.9	78.8
Rubber and electrical equipment	80.6	99.9	58.6
Extractive industries[1]	91.3	99.7	62.5
Chemicals	100.0	100.0	45.3
Paper and board	100.0	100.0	63.0
Plastics	100.0	100.0	67.4
Total	90.5	99.7	68.3

[1] See "La diffusione del lavoro a squadra nella industria
italiana", in Rassegna di Statistiche del Lavoro (Rome), Nos. 1-3,
1969, pp. 45-48. That article contains information on the
technical aspects of the survey.

[2] Including petroleum, quarries and marble.

2. Proportion of workers operating under the
various shift systems in certain
branches of industry

Branches of industry	2 x 8	3 x 8	Continuous cycle	Total
Metallurgy (a) (b)	45.9 55.4	11.7 14.1	25.3 30.5	82.9 100.0
Engineering (a) (b)	57.1 72.5	21.0 26.7	0.6 0.8	78.7 100.0
Rubber and electrical equip. (a) (b)	30.0 51.3	26.4 45.1	2.1 3.6	58.5 100.0
Extractive industries[1] (a) (b)	36.7 58.8	15.2 24.3	10.5 16.9	62.4 100.0
Chemicals (a) (b)	4.4 9.7	2.8 6.1	38.1 84.2	45.3 100.0
Paper and board (a) (b)	1.9 3.0	28.3 45.0	32.8 52.0	63.0 100.0
Plastics (a) (b)	15.3 22.7	45.2 67.0	6.9 10.3	67.4 100.0
All branches (a) (b)	40.6 59.7	16.5 24.2	11.0 16.1	68.1 100.0

[1] Including petroleum, quarries and marble.

(a) Per 100 workers employed.
(b) Per 100 workers on shift work.

Japan

The Ministry of Labour published, in 1968, the findings of a survey of wages and systems of hours of work for 1967[1], which included information on shift work. Some of that information is given in the following three tables.

---

[1] The main findings of this survey have been translated into English by the Branch Office of the ILO in Tokyo for the purposes of this study. Two other surveys on the same subject were conducted in 1965 and 1966; the results are given in Ministry of Labour, Labour Statistics and Research Division: Year Book of Labour Statistics (in Japanese and English) for those years.

1. Establishments where work was done in shifts (all branches of economic activity; by size of establishment), 1968

Establishments employing -	Per cent in which shift work is done
5,000 persons and above	34.0
1,000 to 4,999 persons	26.7
500 to 999 persons	27.9
100 to 499 persons	22.9
30 to 99 persons	16.7
All establishments	20.0

2. Percentage of workers by size of establishment and by shift system, 1968

Establishments employing	No shift work	Two shifts	Three shifts	Continuous 24-hour working	Other shift systems
5,000 persons and above	62.9	17.3	18.3	0.7	0.8
1,000 to 4,999 persons	64.8	17.6	14.8	1.0	1.8
500 to 999 persons	64.5	23.1	10.2	1.7	0.5
100 to 499 persons	63.9	19.6	7.3	7.3	1.9
30 to 99 persons	59.1	23.5	7.7	7.6	2.1
All establishments	63.1	19.4	12.5	3.5	1.5

It should be noted that the system now widely used in most countries, whereby a fourth crew is introduced into the continuous 3 x 8 system, is only just coming into use in Japan. It will be remembered that this reduces the weekly hours of work of members of each shift.

3. Number of workers in establishments where shift work had been introduce, 1968

Industry	Percentage of workers in these establishments, as compared with the total number in the branch concerned	Percentage of workers in these establishments on shift work	Of the workers on shift work, percentage[1] working		
			a two-shift system	a semi-continuous three-shift system	a continuous three-shift shift
All industries	39.0	37.0	53.0	34.0	9.0
Manufacturing industries	47.2	33.0	60.0	36.0	1.5
Food and kindred products	29.0	31.0	66.0	29.0	2.0
Pulp, paper and paper-allied products	54.0	49.0	6.6	93.0	0.2
Publishing, printing and allied industries	35.0	37.0	38.0	12.0	18.0
Rubber products	67.0	27.0	30.0	65.0	0.7
Ceramics, stone and clay products	61.0	26.0	39.0	57.0	3.0
Fabricated metal products	24.0	17.0	85.0	12.0	1.0
Precision machinery	14.0	2.0	69.0	9.0	16.0

1 The sum of the percentages does not always equal 100, since it includes "other answers" not mentioned in the table.

United Kingdom

Two inquiries were conducted, at an interval of nine years (1954-1964), by the Ministry of Labour.[1]   The statistics published give the proportion of wage earners on shift work in industry.

1. **Percentage of industrial wage earners on shift work, 1954 and 1964**

	1954	1964
All industry groups[2]	12.0	18.0
Manufacturing industries	12.0	20.0

2. **Percentage of wage earners on shift work in major industry groups, 1954 and 1964**

Industry group	1954	1964
Vehicles	13.0	33.0
Engineering and electrical goods	7.0	11.0
Paper, printing and publishing	14.0	24.0
Textiles	11.0	22.0

3. **Percentage of wage earners on shift work by shift system, for all industry groups, 1954 and 1964**

	Three shifts	Two day shifts	Alternate day and night	Permanent night	Evening
1954	48.0	16.0	23.0	9.0	4.0
1964	41.0	17.0	23.0	12.0	7.0

---

[1] Published in Ministry of Labour Gazette (London), Vol. 62, No. 10, Oct. 1954, pp. 337-342, and Vol. 73, No. 4, Apr. 1965, pp. 148-155.   See the articles in question for the definitions of the various shift work systems as well as the scope and technical characteristics of each of the inquiries.

[2] All manufacturing industries plus mining and quarrying (except coal), provision of gas, electricity and water, and miscellaneous services (laundries, dry cleaning, motor repairers and repair of boots and shoes).

5. Selected Bibliography

I. General Surveys and
   Sociological Studies

ANDERSEN, A. F. J. E. : Treskiftsarbejde en social-medicinsk
undersøgelse, Social forsknings instituttet, Publication No. 42
(Copenhagen, Kommission hos teknisk forlag, 1970). Vols. 1 and
2, 336 and 277 pp. English summary in Vol. 2.

ARLIAUD, M. : Recherche préparatoire à une sociologie du "travail
noir", Diplomes d'études supérieures de la faculté des lettres et
des sciences humaines (Aix-en-Provence, Université d'Aix-Marseille,
1965). 128 pp. + bibliography.

BAST, G. H. : Ploegenarbeid in de industrie (Arnhem, Contractgroepvereniging Produktiviteit, Van Loghum Staterus, 1960).

ILO : Shift work and ILO, General Conditions of Work Series, No. 2
(Geneva, 1967; mimeographed). 28 pp.

COOK, F. P. : Shift work (London, Institute of Personnel Management,
1954). 36 pp.

DANKERT, Clyde E., MANN, Floyd C., and NORTHRUP, Herbert R. :
Hours of work (New York, Harper and Row, 1965). viii + 208 pp.

DOWNIE, J. H. : Some social and industrial implications of shift
work (London, Industrial Welfare Society (IWS), 1963).

FOURASTIÉ, Jean : La productivité, Collection "Que sais-je?"
(Paris, Presses universitaires de France, 1962). 120 pp.

FRIEDMANN, Georges : Le travail en miettes, Spécialisation et
loisirs (Paris, Gallimard, 1964). 347 pp.

_____ "Le loisir et la civilisation technicienne", Aspects
sociologiques du loisir, Revue internationale des sciences
sociales (Paris), Vol. XII, No. 4, 1960, pp. 556 et seq.

GROSSIN, William : Le travail et le temps: horaires, durées,
rythmes, une enquête dans la construction mécanique et électrique
dans la région parisienne (Paris, Anthropos, 1969). 248 pp.

MAURICE, Marc and MONTEIL, Collette : Vie quotidienne et horaires
de travail, Enquête psychosociologique sur le travail en équipes
successives (Paris, Université, Institut des sciences sociales
du travail, 1965). 279 pp. + Appendices.

MINISTRY OF LABOUR (United Kingdom) : Introduction of shift
working, A survey (London, HM Stationery Office, 1967). v + 26 pp.

MOTT, P. E , MANN, F. C., McLOUGHLIN, Q., and WARWICK, D. :
Shift work The social, psychological and physical consequences
(Ann Arbor University of Michigan Press, 1965). vi + 351 pp.

NAVILLE, P erre : Vers l'automatisme social? Problèmes du travail
et de l'au omation (Paris, Gallimard, 1963). 262 pp.

          et al.: <u>L'automation et le travail humain</u>, Rapport
d'enquête, France 1957-1959 (Paris, Conseil national de la
recherche scientifique, 1961).   750 pp.

NEULOH, Otto; BRAUN, Rudolf, and WERNER, Erich : <u>Die durchlaufende</u>
<u>Arbeitsweise</u>, Sonntagsarbeit im Urteil der Stahlarbeiter
(Tübingen, J. C. B. Mohr, 1961).   300 pp.

ILO, Chemical Industries Committee, Third Session, Geneva, 1952,
Report III : <u>General problems of hours of work in the chemical</u>
<u>industries, with particular reference to a comparison of day work</u>
<u>and shift work</u> (Geneva, ILO, 1952; mimeographed).   iv + 98 pp.

                    Sixth Session, Geneva, 1962, Report III :
<u>Principles and methods for determining extra rates for shift work</u>
<u>and overtime in the chemical industries</u> (Geneva, ILO, 1962;
mimeographed).   iii + 119 pp.

PARSONS, Talcott : <u>The social system</u> (Glencoe (Illinois), The
Free Press, 1951).   xviii + 575 pp.

RHEE, H. A. : <u>Office automation in social perspective</u>, The progress
and social implications of electronic data processing (Oxford,
Basil Blackwell, 1968).   242 pp.

SOROKIN : <u>Sociocultural causality, space, time</u> (London, Cambridge
University Press, 1943).   ix + 246 pp.

TOURAINE, A. : <u>La societé postindustrielle</u> (Paris, Denoël, 1969).
315 pp.

VILLIGER, Armin : <u>Entwicklung und soziale Probleme der industriellen</u>
<u>Schichtarbeit, insbesondere in der Schweiz</u> (Winterthur, Verlag Hans
Schellenberg, 1967).

II.   Technical, Economic and
      Social Aspects

ALEXANDER, K. J. W., and SPRAOS, John : "Shift working : An
application of the theory of the firm", in <u>Quarterly Journal of</u>
<u>Economics</u> (Cambridge, Massachusetts), Vol. 70, November 1956.

ASHER, B. : "The future of shift working", in <u>The benefits and</u>
<u>problems of shift working</u>, A PERA symposium, 7th and 8th June 1966,
section 10 (London, Production Engineering Research Association
of Great Britain (PERA), 1966).

BANKS, Olive : <u>The attitudes of steelworkers to technical change</u>
(Liverpool University Press, 1960).   viii + 152 pp.

                    "Continuous shift work; The attitudes of wives",
in <u>Occupational Psychology</u> (London, National Institute of
Industrial Psychology), Vol. 30, No. 2, April 1956, pp. 69-84.

BANNISTER, J. A. : "The impact of shift working on management" in
<u>The benefits and problems of shift working</u>, A PERA symposium, 7th
and 8th June 1966, section 3 (London, PERA, 1966).

BLAKELOCK, E. : "A new look at the new leisure", in Administrative Science Quarterly (Ithaca (New York)), No. 4, 1960, pp. 446-467.

BROWN, Hilda G. : Some effects of shift work on social and domestic life, Occasional Paper No. 2 (Hull, University Department of Economics and Commerce, 1959). 54 pp.

CAILLOT, R. : "Conséquences sociales du travail à feu continu", in Economie et humanisme (Caluire), No. 122, 1959, pp. 62-72.

CHOMBART DE LAUWE, P. : La vie quotidienne des familles ouvrières (Paris, Conseil national de la recherche scientifique, 1956). 308 pp.

COMMUNAUTE ECONOMIQUE EUROPEENNE : Les salaires dans les branches d'industrie, Etudes, série politique sociale, Nos. 10 and 12 (Brussels, 1965 and 1966).

_____ Le travail dominical dans les Etats membres de la CEE, Etudes, série politique et sociale, No. 17 (Brussels, 1967). 124 pp.

COMMUNAUTE EUROPEENNE DU CHARBON ET DE L'ACIER (CECA) : Etude des travaux continus et semi-continus dans l'industrie sidérurgique de la Communauté (situation au 30 juin 1962) (Luxembourg, CECA, 1962).

DANKERT, Clyde E. : "Shorter hours and multiple shifts : A future pattern?", in Personnel (New York), Vol. XXXVI, 1959, pp. 61-69.

DE JONG, J. R. : "Economische en technische aspecten van ploegenarbeid", in Mens en Onderneming (Groningen), No. 12, pp. 338-346.

FEDERATION INTERNATIONALE DES SYNDICATE CHRETIENS D'INDUSTRIES DIVERSES : Informations (La Haye), No. 1, 1964.

GREENBAUM, Marcia L. : The shorter workweek, Bulletin No. 50 (Ithaca, New York, Cornell University, June 1963). 52 pp.

GROSSIN, William : "Temps-machines, temps-hommes", Quelques résultats d'une enquête sur l'automation, Cahiers d'étude de l'automation et des societés industrielles (Paris, Conseil national de la recherche scientifique), No. 4, 1962, pp. 171-188.

INDUSTRIAL WELFARE SOCIETY : Shift work, Summaries of papers and discussion at a one-day conference held on 4th December 1963, Information Survey and Report Series, No. 112 (London, 1963). 36 pp. + appendices.

KABAJ, M. : "Shift work and employment expansion", in International Labour Review, Vol. 91, No. 1, January 1965, pp. 47-62.

_____ "Shift work and employment expansion : towards an optimum pattern", ibid., Vol. 98, No. 3, September 1968, pp. 245-274.

LIPSET, Seymour Martin, TROW, Martin A., and COLEMAN, James S. : Union democracy: The internal politics of the International Typographical Union (Glencoe, Illinois, The Free Press, 1956). 455 pp.

LUCAS, A. : "L'automation à la Régie Renault", in Economie et humanisme (Caluire), No. 112, July-August 1958, pp. 245-256.

MANN, Floyd A. : "Shift work and the shorter workweek", in Dankert, Clyde E., Mann, Floyd C., and Northrup, Herbert R. : Hours of work (New York, Harper and Row, 1965), pp. 111-127.

            and HOFFMANN, L. Richard : Automation and the worker (New York, Henry Holt, 1960). xiv + 272 pp.

MARRIS, Robin : "The economics of shift working", in The benefits and problems of shift working, A PERA symposium, 7th and 8th June 1966, section 6 (London, PERA, 1966).

            et al : The economics of capital utilisation, A report on multiple shift work, University of Cambridge, Department of Applied Economics, Monographs, No. 10 (London, Cambridge University Press, 1964). 267 pp.

MAURICE, Marc, and MONTEIL, Collette: "Le travail continue en équipes successives", in Revue française du travail (Paris, Ministère du Travail), 18th year, Nos. 3-4, July-December 1964, pp. 5-31.

            Vie quotidienne et horaires de travail, Enquête psychosociologique sur le travail en équipes successives (Paris, Université, Institut des sciences sociales du travail, 1965). 279 pp + appendices.

MOTT, F. E., MANN, Floyd C., McLOUGHLIN, Q., and WARWICK, D. : Shift work: The social, psychological and physical consequences (Ann Arbor, University of Michigan Press, 1965). vi + 351 pp.

ORGANISATION EUROPEENNE DE COOPERATION ECONOMIQUE (EX-), AGENCE EUROPEENNE DE PRODUCTIVITE : Travailleurs de l'acier et progrès technique, Rapport comparatif sur six enquêtes nationales (Paris, OECE, 1959). 70 pp.

PIGORS, P. and F. : Human aspects of multiple shift operations, Department of Economic and Social Science, Series 2, No. 13 (Cambridge (Massachusetts), Massachusetts Institute of Technology, 1944), 90 pp.

POWELL, D. C. : "Flexibility in shift working: Alternative methods", in The benefits and problems of shift working, A PERA symposium, 7th and 8th June 1966, section 8 (London, PERA, 1966).

PRODUCTION ENGINEERING RESEARCH ASSOCIATION (PERA) : The benefits and problems of shift working, A PERA symposium, 7th and 8th June 1966 (London, PERA, 1966).

SCANLON, H. : "The trade union viewpoint", in The benefits and problems of shift working, op. cit., section 2.

SHEPHERD, R. D., and WALKER, J. : "Three-shift working and the distribution of absence", in Occupational Psychology (London), No. 30, 1956, pp. 105-111.

TOWERS, J. M. : "Shift working: A review of British and foreign patterns", in The benefits and problems of shift working, op. cit., section 1.

ULICH, E. : "Zur Frage der Belastung des arbeitenden Menschen durch Nacht- und Schichtarbeit", in Psychologische Rundschau (Göttingen), No. 1, 1957, pp. 57-59.

WILENSKY, H. L. : "The moonlighter", in Industrial Relations (Berkeley, California), Vol. 3, No. 1, October 1963.

WISNER, A. : "Shift work and night work", Labor (Brussels, International Federation of Christian Trade Unions), 31st Year, Nos. 5-8, May-August 1958, pp. 154-156.

WYATT, S., and MARRIOTT, R. : "Night work and shift changes", in British Journal of Industrial Medicine (London, British Medical Association), Vol. 10, No. 3, July 1953, pp. 164-172.

III. Medical, Physiological and
      Psychological Aspects

AANONSEN, A. : "Medical problems of shift work", in Industrial Medicine and Surgery (Oslo), No. 28, 1959, pp. 422-427.

———————— Shift work and health (Oslo, Universitetsforlaget, 1964), 96 pp.

ANDERSEN, E. J. : "The main results of the Danish medico-psychosocial investigation of shiftworkers", in Publications du XIIe Congrès international de médecine du travail, Helsinki, 1-6 July 1957 (Helsinki, 1958), Vol. III: Travaux, pp. 135-136.

ANDLAUER, P. : "La variation de fréquence horaire des accidents du travail dans les industries à feu continu", in Le travail humain (Paris, Presses universitaires de France, XVIIIth Year, 1955), pp. 193-222.

———————— and FOURRE, L. : Aspects ergonomiques du travail en équipes alternantes (Strasbourg, Centre d'études de physiologie appliquée au travail, 1962). 168 pp.

———————— and METZ, B. : "Le travail en équipes alternantes", in SCHERRER, J. (ed.): Physiologie du travail (ergonomie) (Paris, Masson et Cie, 1967).

BJERNER, B., HOLM and SWENSSON, A. : "Diurnal variation in mental performance", in British Journal of Industrial Medicine (London), No. 12, 1955.

———————— and SWENSSON, A. : "Schichtarbeit und Rhythmus", in Acta Medica Scandinavica (Stockholm), Supplement No. 278, 1953, pp. 102-107.

BONJER, F. H. : "Physiological aspects of shiftwork", in Publications du XIIIe Congrès international de médecine du travail, New York, 25-29 July 1960 (New York, 1961), Proceedings, pp. 848-849.

BROWN, Hilda G. : Some effects of shift work on social and domestic life, Occasional Paper No. 2 (Hull University, Department of Economics and Commerce, 1959). 54 pp.

BRUSGAARD, A. : Medizinske vurderinger av såkalt helseskadelig arbeid, saerlig skiftarbeid (Oslo, 1949).

BURGER, G. C. E., VAN ALPHEN DE VEER, M. R., GROOT WESSELDIJK, A. Th., v. d. GRAAF, M. H. K., and DOORNBOSCH, A. : "Human problems in shift work", in Publications du XIIe Congrès international de médecine du travail, Helsinki, 1-6 July 1957 (Helsinki, 1958), Vol. III: Travaux, pp. 126-128.

CAILLOT, R. : "Conséquences sociales du travail à feu continu", in Economie et humanisme (Caluire), No. 122, 1959, pp. 62-72.

CASTELNUEVO-TEDESCO : "Emotional antecedents of perforation of ulcers of the stomach and duodenum", in Psychosomatic Medicine (New York), Vol. 24, No. 4, 1968, pp. 398-416.

DE LA MARE, G., and WALKER, J. : "Shift working: The arrangement of hours on night work", in Nature (London), No. 208, 1965, pp. 1127-1128.

DERVILLEE, P., and LAZARINI, H. J. : "A propos du travail en équipe avec changement d'horaires. Incidences familiales et répercussion possible sur la santé des travailleurs", in Archives des maladies professionnelles de médecine du travail et de sécurité sociale (Paris), Vol. 20, 1959, pp. 306-309.

ERANKO, O. : "25-hour day: One solution to the shift work problem", in Publications du XIIe Congrés international de médecine du travail, Helsinki, 1-6 July 1957 (Helsinki, 1958), Vol. III: Travaux, pp. 134-135.

FARMER, Eric : A comparison of different shift systems in the glass trade (London, Medical Research Council, 1924). iv + 24 pp.

GRAF, P. : "Zur Frage der Arbeits- und Pausengestattung bei Fliessarbeit", Arbeitsphysiologie (Berlin), No. 12, 1942.

HADENGNE, A., REYNAUD, J. D., and REINBERG, A. : "Les incidences psychophysiologiques et les aspects pathologiques de la répartition des horaires de travail", in VIIes Journées nationales de médecine du travail, September 1962 (Paris, Masson et Cie, 1962).

HEALTH OF MUNITION WORKERS COMMITTEE : Industrial health and efficiency, Final Report, Cmd. 9065 (London, HM Stationery Office, 1918).

HEIDRICH, Z., PASZKOWSKI, W., and WITKOWSKA, H. : Wydajność robotników w krotkich przedzialach czasu pracy (Warsaw, Institute for Social Studies, 1966). 236 pp. With summaries in English, French and German.

HOGG, W. A. : "Shift work, a hazard to health?", in British Medical Bulletin (London), No. 21, 1961, pp. 2-21.

JARDILLER, P. : "L'avenir de la psychologie industrielle" in Travail humain (Paris, Presses universitaires de France), No. 24, 1960.

KLEITMAN, N. : "Biological rhythms and cycles", in Physiological Reviews (Baltimore, American Physiological Society), No. 29, 1949, pp. 1-30.

_____ Sleep and wakefulness (Chicago University Press, 1939). 638 pp.

KOSSORIS : "Studies of the effects of long working hours", in Monthly Labor Review (Washington), October 1944, p. 1738.

KUBLER, G. : Variations périodiques de la fréquence et de la gravité des accidents du travail dans plusieurs industries à travail continu, Thèse de doctorat de la faculté de médecine (Strasbourg, 1956), 36 pp.

LOBBAN, M. C., and TREDRE, B. E. : "Daily rhythms of renal extraction in human subjects with irregular hours of work", Journal of Physiology (London, Physiological Society of Great Britain), No. 38, 1966, pp. 203-214.

MAURICE, Marc, and MONTEIL, Colette : Vie quotidienne et horaires de travail, Enquête psychosociologique sur le travail en équipes successives (Paris, Université, Institut des sciences sociales du travail, 1965). 279 pp. + appendices.

McGIRR, Owen : "Health considerations", in The benefits and problems of shift working, op. cit., section 5.

MENZEL, W. : Le rhythme nycthémeral de l'homme et le travail par postes alternés (Bale, Benno Schwabe, 1962).

METZ, B., and SIGWALT, D. : "Variations nycthémerales des effets physiologiques du travail musculaire et de la chaleur ambiante", in Archives des sciences physiologiques (Paris), No. 12, 1958, pp. 301-380.

MURREL, K. F. H. : Ergonomics: Man in his working environment (London, Chapman and Hall, 1965). xviii + 496 pp.

NATIONAL INDUSTRIAL CONFERENCE BOARD : Night work in industry (New York, 1927). ix + 45 pp.

PARDON, M. N. : "Des horaires de travail", in Archives des maladies professionnelles, de médecine du travail et de sécurité sociale (Paris, Masson), Vol. 19, No. 4, July-August 1958, pp. 391-394.

PIERACH, A. : "Biological rhythm effects of night work and shift changes on the health of workers", in Acta Medica Scandinavica (Stockholm), Supplement No. 307, Vol. CLII, 1955.

SARTIN, P. : La fatigue industrielle, comment humaniser le travail (Paris, Societé auxiliaire pour la diffusion des éditions de productivité, 1960). 238 pp.

TELEKY, L. : "Problems of night work: influences on health and efficiency", in Industrial Medicine (Chicago), Vol. XII, No. 11, November 1943, pp. 758-779.

THIIS-EVENSEN, E. : "Shift work and health", in Industrial Medicine (Chicago), Vol. XXVII, 1958, pp. 493-497.

ULICH, E. Schicht- und Nachtarbeit in Betrieb, Rationalisierungs-kuratorium der deutschen Wirtschaft (Cologne and Opladen, Westdeutscher Verlag, 1964). 66 pp.

_____ "Zur Frage der Belastung des arbeitende Menschen durch Nacht- und Schichtarbeit", in Physiologische Rundschau (Göttingen), No. 1, 1957, pp. 57-59.

VAN LOON, J. H. : "Diurnal body temperature curves in shift workers", in Ergonomics (London), No. 6, 1963, pp. 267-273.

VEIL, Cl. : "Rapport sur les rhythmes de travail", Journées de la santé mentale (Paris, 1956), in Hygiène mentale (Paris), Vol. XLVI, 1956.

VERNON, H. M. : Hours of work and their influence on health and efficiency (London, British Association for Labour Legislation, 1943).

_____ "Hours of work in wartime", in Personnel Management (London), December 1939.

WALKER, J. : "Frequent alternation of shifts on continuous work", in Occupational Psychology (London), Vol. 40, 1966, pp. 215-225.

_____ "Shift changes and hours of work", ibid., Vol. 35, Nos. 1-2, January-April 1961, pp. 1-9.

WEDDERBURN, A. A. I. : "Social factors in satisfaction with swiftly rotating shifts", ibid., Vol. 41, 1967, pp. 85-107.

WILKINSON, R. T. : "Sleep and dreams", in FOSS, B. M. (ed.): New horizons in psychology (London, Penguin Books, 1966).

WYATT, S., and MARRIOTT, R. : "Night work and shift changes", in British Journal of Industrial Medicine (London, British Medical Association), Vol. 10, No. 3, July 1953, pp. 164-172.

_____ et al. : A study of attitudes to factory work, Medical Research Council Special Report Series, No. 292 (London, HM Stationery Office, 1956), 115 pp.

IV. Examples of the Organisation of
    Shift Work

COOK, F. P. : Shift Work (London, Institute of Personnel Management, 1954), pp. 31-33.

HEALY, Williams, C. : "Shift scheduling made easy", in Factory (New York), Vol. 117, No. 10, October 1959, pp. 87-91.

INDUSTRIAL WELFARE SOCIETY : Shift work: Current practice in Great Britain, Information Survey and Report Series, No. 140 (London, 1966).

NORTHRUP, Herbert, R. : Shift problems and practices, Studies in Personnel policy, No. 118 (New York, National Industrial Conference Board, 1951), 23 pp.

_____ : Shift schedules for continuous operations (Princeton University Press, 1943).

STANFORD UNIVERSITY, GRADUATE SCHOOL OF BUSINESS : Shift schedules in continuous process industries (Stanford University Press, 1942), 42 pp.

TAYLOR, E. E. D. : "Shift working", in Personnel Management (London), Information series No. 3, 1967.